SPITFIRE EVOLUTION

PAUL BEAVER
ARTWORK BY JON FREEMAN • FOREWORD BY DAVID FADDY

Dedicated to the men and women of Supermarine and its contractors who created, developed and evolved the Spitfire into the greatest icon in aviation history.

© Paul Beaver & Beaver Westminster Ltd 2016
Artwork © Jon Freeman 2016

ISBN 978-0-9935545-0-6

All Rights Reserved. No part of this publication may be reproduced or stored in a retrieval system or transmitted, in any form or by any means, electronic, mechanical. Photocopying, recording or otherwise, without prior permission in writing from Beaver Westminster Ltd.

Published in March 2016 to commemorate the 80th Anniversary of the first flight of the Supermarine Type 300 which became the 'Spitfire'.

Published by Beaver Westminster Ltd
45 Great Peter Street, London SW1P 3LT

Printed & Bound by Bulpitt Print Ltd

Every effort has been made to trace and acknowledge holders of copyright on material herein and the publisher and the author assume no responsibility for any errors or omissions, nor liability for damages resulting from the use if this information.

Designed by Richard Parsons
Historical Research by Jack Beaver
Edited by Cate Pye and John Davis

www.paulbeaver.org

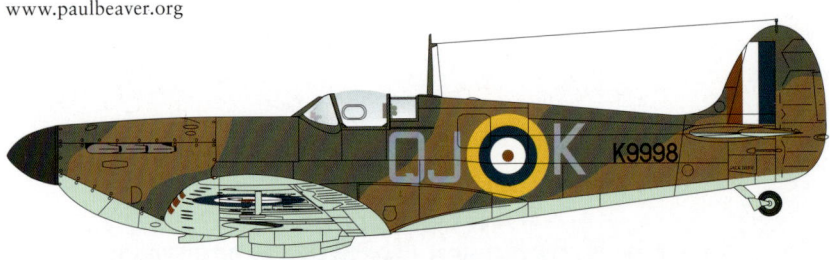

CONTENTS

Foreword by David Faddy	4
Introduction	6
The Legend is Born	8
Adolescence	10
Experience Counts	14
Evolutionary Back Water	16
Early spies in the sky	17
Overmatching	22
Floatplane	26
Spitfire pressurised	27
High Flyer	28
Superb Dogfighter	32
Wing profiles	36
Two-seat trainers	43
Faster spy in the sky	46
Ultimate Merlins	48
Enter the Griffon	50
XVIII redesign	52
Last Act	54
Finale	56
Evolving Webbed Feet	60
Adapting the Spitfire	64
Enter the Griffon II	66
Interim Griffon Seafire	68
Ultimate & Definitive	70
Acknowledgements	72

FOREWORD
DAVID FADDY

I am pleased to introduce this book on the Spitfire's Evolution. It helps to shine light into the engineering side of the design for which Supermarine and the British aircraft industry rightly receives global recognition.

In the previous book, *Spitfire People*, Paul Beaver highlighted the characters who were so important to the Supermarine Spitfire. He calls them 'unsung heroes' and he is right to do so. I have always believed that my father, Alf Faddy, is one of those unsung for far too long.

The Spitfire was the first British aircraft in which the stresses were carried in the skin and not in a separate internal structure. My father travelled around Fighter Command airfields and Maintenance Units during the war to supervise repairs after battle damage. He discovered that these repairs were sometimes achieved by pop riveting biscuit tin lids over the bullet holes – which adversely affected the strength of the structure!

Aircraft of the Spitfire generation could not be designed by a single individual; many different skills were required. The design of the Spitfire was the work of a team. Engineers of that generation, which included RJ Mitchell, Joe Smith and Alf Faddy, had served apprenticeships in the railways or ship

Prince Philip visited Supermarine on 17 April 1953 and was shown around by Joe Smith, by then Chief Designer (centre) and Alf Faddy (centre, light suit). Other visible, standing back, are Hew Kilner and Chief Test Pilot, Jeffrey Quill.

building. They also needed the support of the people with the academic skills of aerodynamics, structural design, metallurgy and so on.

In 1917, at the age of 22, Mitchell joined Supermarine, which had been founded by Noel Pemberton Billing in 1913, initially as personal assistant to Hubert Scott-Paine who had taken over ownership of the company from its founder. Both Mitchell and Faddy were, the words of the Vickers' obituary on the latter, products of the time when aircraft engineering was largely a matter of experience and flair". Indeed, Alf Faddy retained a degree of scepticism about, perhaps even a slight contempt for, people who had not served an engineering apprenticeship but came into aeronautics via university degrees.

Knowing that Alf Faddy had significant aircraft design experience, Mitchell invited him to join Supermarine in 1930. He was a little older than his contemporaries; he was meticulous to the extreme; never satisfied with anything less than the best. He became the Spitfire Structural Design Section Leader. He used to say "draw with the pencil but design with the rubber". Schemes prepared with his guidance were always revised at least once but usually more often. Thus the outstanding basic design concept was matched by meticulous effort in the drawing office. The result was the Spitfire.

After the war my father took me to the High Post airfield to see rows of production Spitfires waiting to be broken up – each with their cockpit instruments sledgehammered to ensure that they not be flown – such a sad sight.

David Faddy, an aeronautical engineer in his early career when he worked at RAE Farnborough on such projects as the world's first digital computer for the TSR-2 weapons system. He later became Assistant Chief Scientific Advisor in the Ministry of Defence. He is the son of Alf Faddy.

INTRODUCTION

Supermarine at Southampton created the world's most iconic aeroplane and, it could be argued, one of the most iconic engineering achievements of the early 20th Century. The engineering achievement was all the more remarkable because it brought together a host of other like-minded people at other world class companies like Rolls-Royce.

The Spitfire story is one of evolution. It takes the basic design of 1938, tripled the all-up weight, puts in a new powerplant, doubled the range, armed it to the teeth and kept it relevant until the jet age. A remarkable story which has been told many times but deserves to be told again – but this time with the excellent art of Jon Freeman to show the more than 60 variants, sub-variants and modifications.

To try and keep the story in chronological order is difficult. So one mark morphs into another within a few months; it might even change engine types and roles. The Spitfire story is one of innovation as well as evolution. Beverley Shenstone's wing served for eight long, war-torn years until speed and structural needs causes a new design. Laminar flow – as fitted to the Mustang – was also tried as technology threatened to over-match piston-engined fighters with jet power.

The Spitfire's supremacy had been challenged before. It had mastered the Bf 109F with the Mk V. When it was bettered by Kurt Tank's Fw 190 in the skies over Flanders in 1941, it took some months to create what was planned to be an interim solution, , the Mk IX. As the Fw 190 was improved, so Supermarine turned to the Griffon engine to give the improved performance needed.

The Griffon gave the Spitfire a new lease of life to both the fighter and the remarkable photo-reconnaissance versions. Structural and range improvements followed but still the Spitfire retained its characteristic look – and therefore appeal even today.

The Spitfire also went to sea, first as a hooked version of the land-based fighter and then as naval versions which followed the development of the Spitfire and ending with the ultimate of the family, the Seafire Mk 47 which saw service in the early months of the Korean War in 1950.

Tracking the Spitfire mark numbers has always been a challenge and one of the main outcomes of this book is that they make sense now, at least to me. In a small book, it has not been possible to cover every angle but I hope that the basics are there. As always, the omissions and errors are mine.

THE LEGEND IS BORN

Supermarine's combined Drawing and Technical Office at Woolston, on the first floor of an Art Deco building situated on the east bank of the River Itchen, across the water from Southampton, was the nerve centre of one of the most innovative aeronautical design houses in the world.

Under the overall leadership of R J Mitchell, the company had pioneered innovation and design in seaplanes and flying boats. In the 1930s, with the success of the Schneider Trophy under its belt, the company moved into the new era of fast, monoplane fighter design.

Supermarine's first attempt, the Type 224, built to win the Air Ministry Specification F7/30 issued in October 1931, was a failure. Although the Air Ministry ordered a prototype of the open cockpit, fixed-undercarriage, cranked wing design, it did not meet the cardinal points of the specification, especially speed and firepower. It was rejected by the Air Ministry. After its first flight on 19 February 1934 and subsequent tests by Vickers' chief test pilot, Mutt Summers, Mitchell became increasingly pre-occupied with the diagnosis of colon cancer. He was also obsessed with his four-engined bomber design which showed great promise and could have rivalled the Lancaster on all performance criteria.

In fact, no contender for Spec F7/30 actually achieved the Air Ministry's desired result of a 300 mph eight-gun monoplane fighter and further

There is no doubt the Schneider trophy racers were instrumental in the Spitfire design; not in shape and form but more in the use of materials and technology.

development money was forthcoming. With its share, Supermarine started work on the Type 300 which brought together every new development and the skills of several highly competent engineers and scientists under the tactical leadership of Alf Faddy and the oversight of Mitchell. It was Faddy who advanced the adoption of Beverley Shenstone's elliptical wing and drew the first designs.

Mitchell attended the first flight of the Type 300 on 5 March 1936, but photographs show clearly that his cancer had taken hold and he took very little part in bringing the prototype through development and into production, preferring to concentrate his last efforts on a high speed amphibian and the Supermarine Type 317 Bomber programmes. Mitchell died on 11 June 1937 but he did live to see the design named 'Spitfire' and the first production contract signed in June 1936, before official testing had been completed.

Supermarine Type 300, Eastleigh
K5054 as she appeared on the afternoon of her first flight
on the afternoon of 5 March 1936.

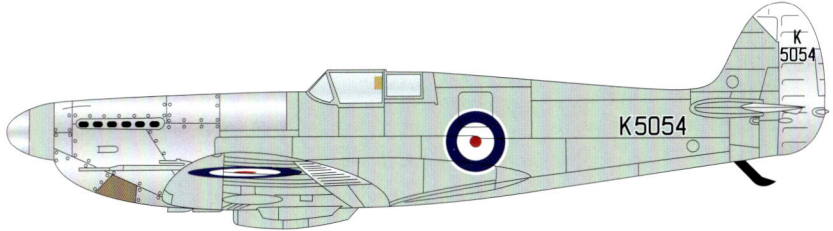

Supermarine Type 300, Martlesham Heath
Hastily camouflaged after Munich, the prototype was destroyed at RAE Farnborough on 4 September 1939, killing Flt Lt Gilbert 'Spinner' White.

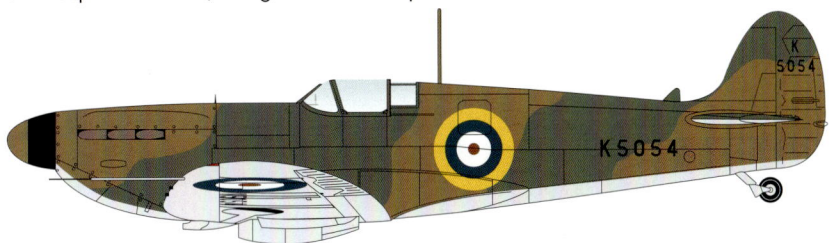

SPITFIRE EVOLUTION **9**

ADOLESCENCE

In January 1937, the fact that Supermarine built aeroplanes as a craft and did not readily understand mass production became clear. The contract called for the first 80 Spitfire Mk I fighters to be ready for Fighter Command. In fact, there were none and it would be December 1937 before the first four production Spitfires were completed; all hand-built. It would take another six months before production testing at Eastleigh, Farnborough and Martlesham Heath was complete and the Air Minister, Lord Swinton was happy to accept the first airframes.

By the time the first squadron was formed at RAF Duxford in August 1938, there were fewer than 50 Spitfires in existence. On 4 August, No 19 officially stood up as a Spitfire squadron and made its first public appearance a few weeks later at the opening of Cambridge Airport.

To evolve production from the level of seaplane hand-built craft products to mass production, Vickers and the Air Ministry called on the expertise of the motor industry, particularly Austin Motors and the Morris Company at Cowley. So concerned was the Minister, Lord Swinton, that he considered

---

Speed Spitfire, Eastleigh

Conscious of the German developments, the Air Ministry and Vickers took a standard Spitfire Mk I from the Woolston production line and modified it for the world speed record in January 1938. Design changes included smaller fuel tanks, a four-bladed Watts propeller and a Merlin II engine. The wingspan was reduced, radiators enlarged and panels smoothed and filled. The speed attempts failed but the Speed Spitfire greatly helped the evolution of the PR Spitfires, becoming a PR Mk II with a variable pitch DH propeller. The small fuel tanks meant it could not be deemed operational and it became a liaison machine, incredibly, being scrapped in 1946.

Spitfire Mk I

K9906, 'FZ.L' flown by Flight Lieutenant Robert Stanford Tuck of No 65 (East India) Squadron, RAF based at RAF Hornchurch, August 1939

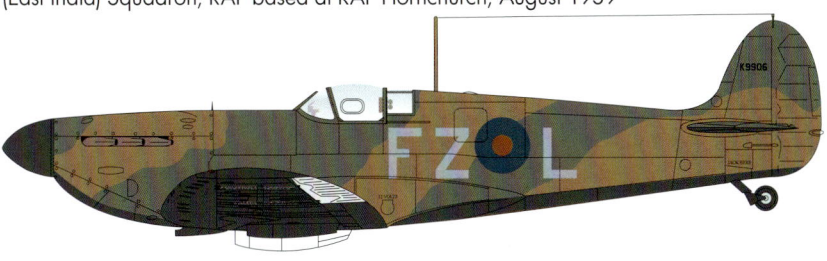

Spitfire Mk IA

P9398, 'KL.B' flown by Pilot Officer Al Deere of No 54 Sqdron, RAF based at RAF Hornchurch, 9 July 1940

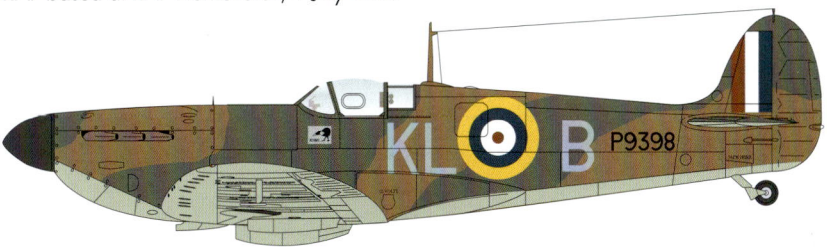

taking Spitfire production away from Supermarine. The company itself also understood the problems and created a series of important sub-assembly contracts which stood the test of time and war emergency. Production evolved through a mixture of understanding what needed to made by Supermarine and what could be created on sub-contractor lines, including the Dispersed Factories and the mass production offered by Castle Bromwich.

Back in the Royal Air Force, at Duxford, Flight Lieutenant Bob Stanford Tuck enters the story of the Spitfire's Evolution at this point. He was one of the nominated service development pilots whose experience and skills from a previous generation's biplane fighters was brought to bear on the Spitfire, helping evolve the Mk I to the Mk Ia. His recommendations included adding height to the rudder pedals, rear view mirror and armed glass.

Key differences between Mk I and Mk Ia – 3-bladed propeller as standard; bulged canopy becoming standard.

PRINCIPAL ITEMS WHOLLY OR PARTIALLY SUB-CONTRACTED

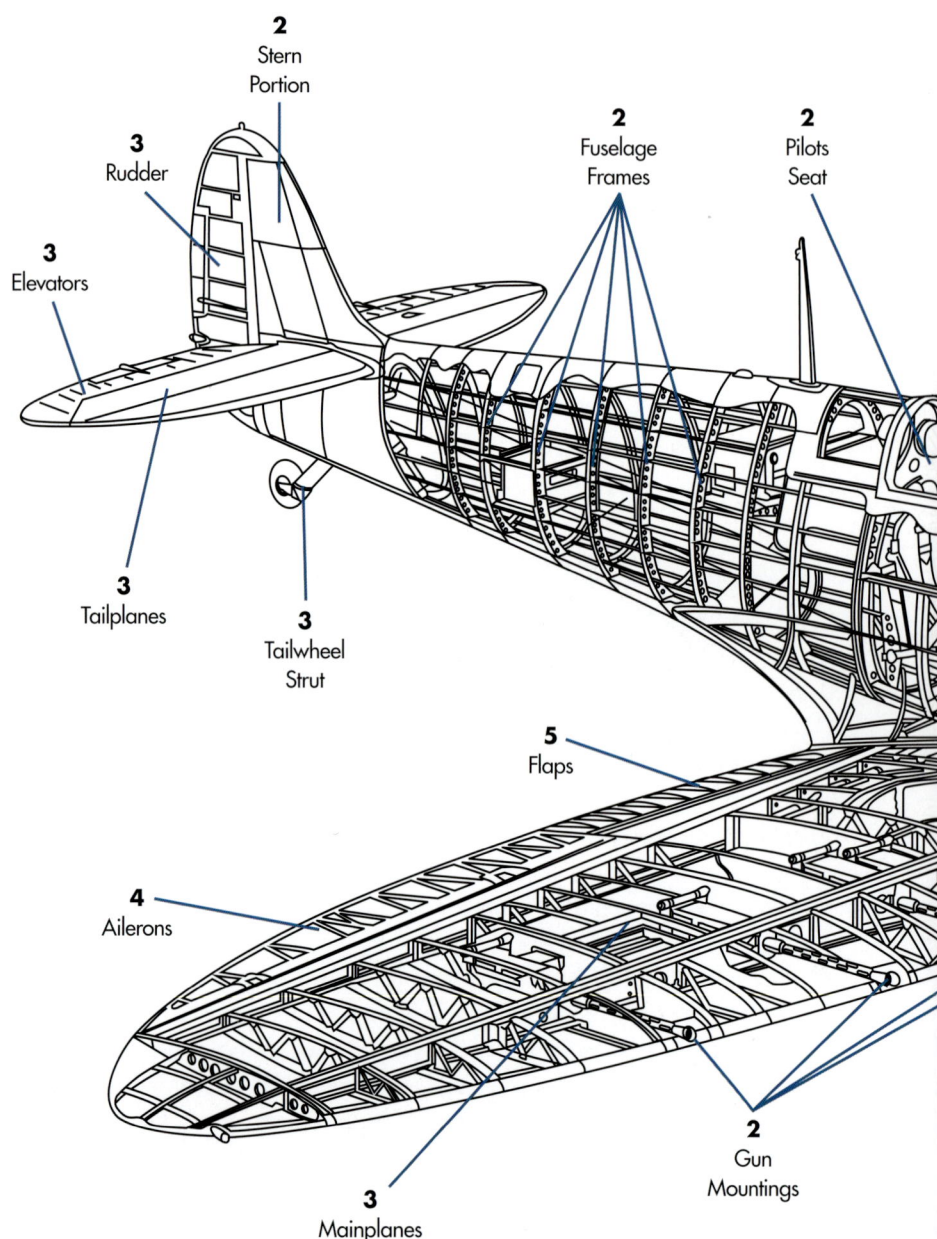

SPITFIRE EVOLUTION

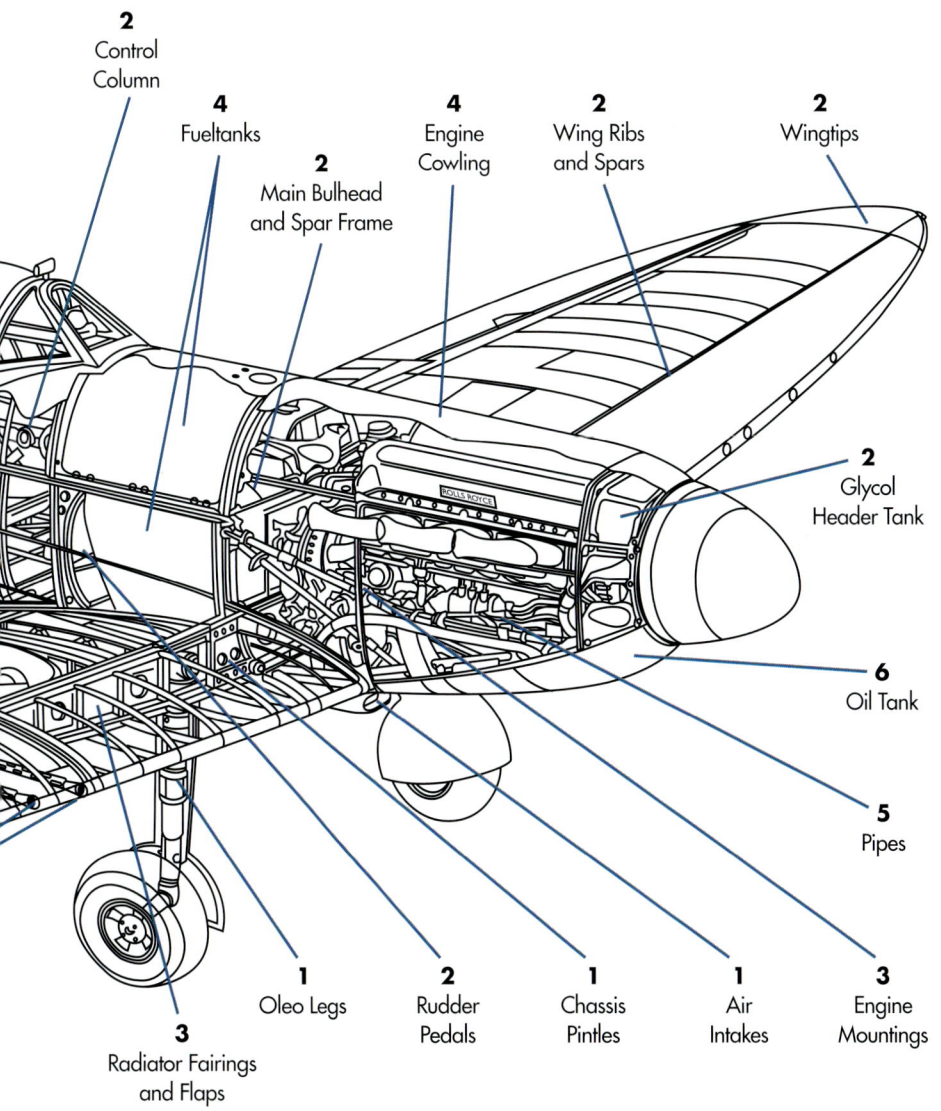

SPITFIRE EVOLUTION

EXPERIENCE COUNTS

Initial Spitfire operations during the Phoney War benefitted from factory-derived upgrades for pilot protection and better performance. First combats against the occasional Heinkel and Dornier bomber showed that the rifle-calibre machine gun was not as effective as first thought.

The opening stages of the Battle of Britain, arguably fought over Flanders during the Dunkirk evacuation, caused not just changes in tactics but also showed where the early Spitfire marks were limited in firepower and performance. This would evolve with combat experience.

Firepower enhancement experiences included fitting Hispano-Suiza cannon and magazines into the Shenstone wing section. It was an

Spitfire Mk IB
R6776, 'QV.H' flown by Flight Sergeant George 'Grumpy' Unwin of No 19 Squadron, RAF based at RAF Fowlmere, August 1940.

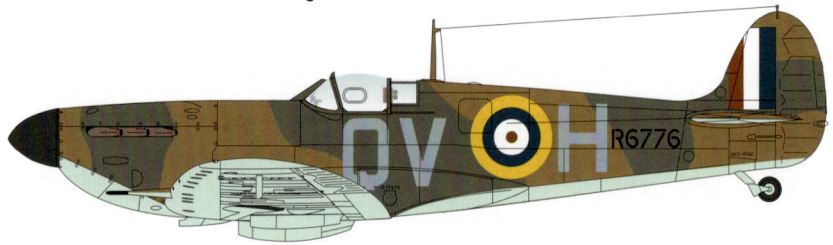

Spitfire Mk IIa
P7895, 'RN.N' flown by Flight Lieutenant R. Deacon Elliot of No 72 (Basutoland) Squadron, RAF based at RAF Acklington, April 1941.

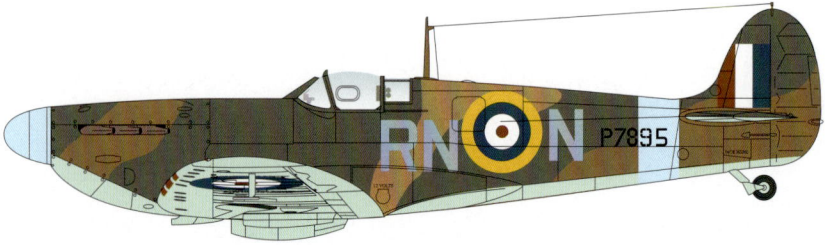

engineering challenge which was not fully resolved until 1941 with space being created by the use of top side fairings on the mainplane in the Mk V.

Cannon-armed Spitfires did fly with No 19 Squadron for a brief period in the summer of 1940. In action, it was clear that cannon had better striking power, especially against bombers but some 'aces' like Douglas Bader still preferred eight machine guns for combat against fighters; hence his choice of the Mk Va when he took command of the Tangmere Wing a year later.

An evolutionary performance dead-end was the delivery of 89 Spitfire Mk II (LR) (some sources say 100) to extend the fighter's range for cross-Channel escort operations in the flawed policy of engaging the *Luftwaffe* over Occupied France. The installation of a fixed tank under the port wing limited agility and caused an asymmetric effect on the controls but the engineering experience was useful for the further evolution of the Spitfire.

Spitfire Mk IIb
P8932, 'ZD.L' of No 222 (Natal) Squadron,
RAF based at RAF Hornchurch, 1941

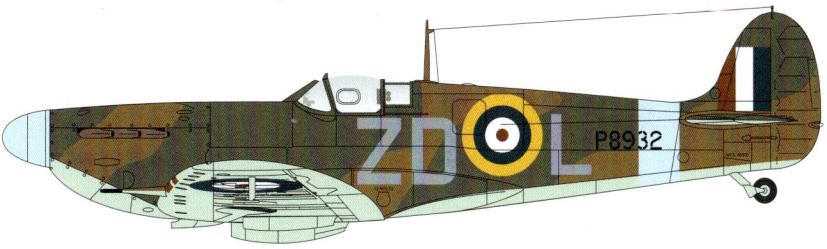

Spitfire Mk II (LR)
P8388, 'UM.R' flown by Flight Sergeant Walt 'Johnnie' Johnston
of No 151 Squadron RAF, August 1941

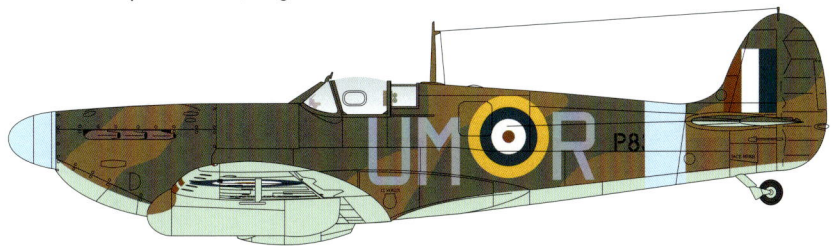

EVOLUTIONARY BACK WATER

Turret Spitfire – the Type 305
In 1935, the Air Ministry planned a two-seat day and night turret fighter which would be capable of engaging fast flying German bombers from below, where they were lightly defended and considered vulnerable. Specification F9/35 was issued to manufacturers, requiring a combat speed of 290 mph at 15,000 feet. Unlike the six rival designs from such companies as Armstrong Whitworth, Boulton Paul, Bristol, Fairey, Gloster and Hawker, the Supermarine offering remained two-seats but the gun turret was not manned. It was hydraulic and electrically-aimed placed in a very similar fuselage to the Type 300 (Spitfire) with a different wing.

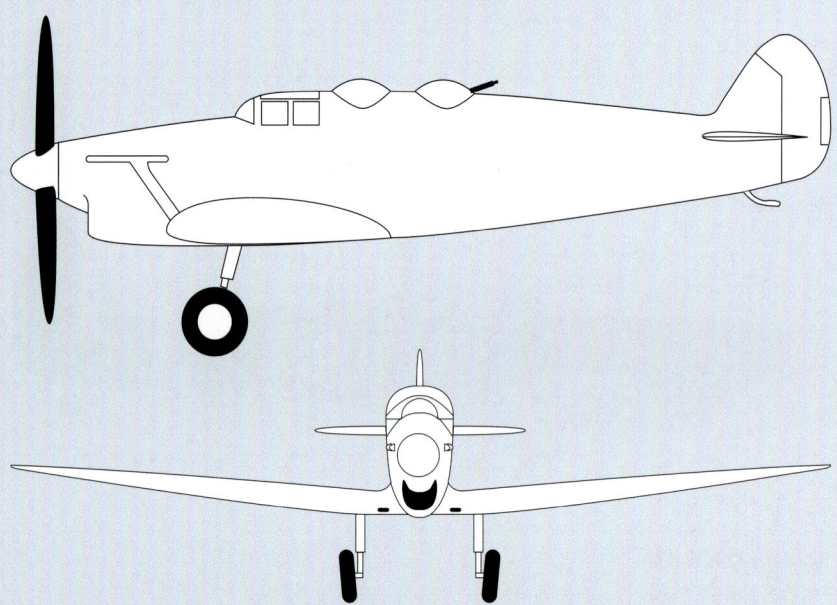

Twin-engined replacement – the Type 324
As early as 1937, Supermarine's design team under Joe Smith and Alf Faddy had looked into the future and planned a replacement for the Spitfire (and the Hurricane). This was a sound idea as technology was making leaps and bounds to counter the growth of Germany. At the same time, the Air Ministry issued Specification F18/37 which was looking for a flush-riveted aluminium alloy skin and powered by the Rolls-Royce Vulture. It did not progress beyond the mock-up stage.

EARLY SPIES IN THE SKY

It is frequently assumed that Spitfires were not based overseas until the Malta deployment in 1941 but from November 1939, prior to the German invasion of France, a small number of Spitfires carried out vital strategic intelligence gathering ranging as far as Aachen from French airfields.

Initially, these were production Mk Is taken straight off the line and sent to Heston where Sidney Cotton's contractor-based PR unit removed guns and faired over the ports, replacing the inner ammunition wells with a vertical 5 inch focal length camera, designated the F24, in each wing. This was designated the Spitfire PR Mk Ia. Later, on upgrade, they were re-designated Mk Ic and later Mk PR III when upgraded.

Spitfire PR Mk Ia
N3071, flown by Flight Lieutenant Maurice 'Shorty' Longbottom of No 2 Camouflage Unit, based at Lile-Seclin, France, 18 November 1939

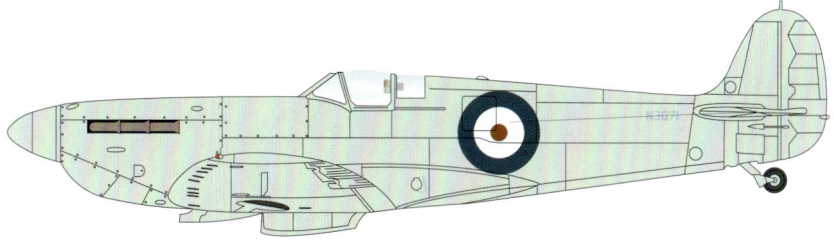

Spitfire PR Mk Ib
P9931 of No 212 Squadron, RAF based at Lille-Seclin, France, spring 1940

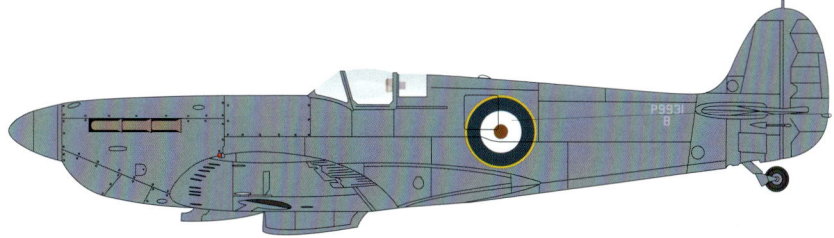

This first upgraded Spitfire was designed the PR Ib and Supermarine fitted a 29 Imp gal tank behind the pilot's position and the photographic deficit was remedied with the 8 inch focal length version of the F24 camera. That put the vital Wilhelmshaven naval base in range by February 1940.

A month later, the Ministry of Aircraft Production authorised 40 airframes to be converted as the PR Mk Ic with a 30 imp gal tank in the port wing and two F24 cameras in the starboard wing, moving a third F24 to the fuselage, aft of the wings. The fact that the wings could be evolved with such modifications is testament to the Shenstone design and the manufacturing skills of companies like General Aircraft, Pobjoy Motors and Pressed Steel.

Evolution was happening at a pace now and design was coping with the additional camera blister, wing and fuselage stresses and higher altitudes. By July 1940, vital inteliigance of German-occupied France was needed

Spitfire PR Mk Ic
R6903, 'LY' flown by Pilot Officer Gordon Green of PRU, RAF St Eval, February 1941

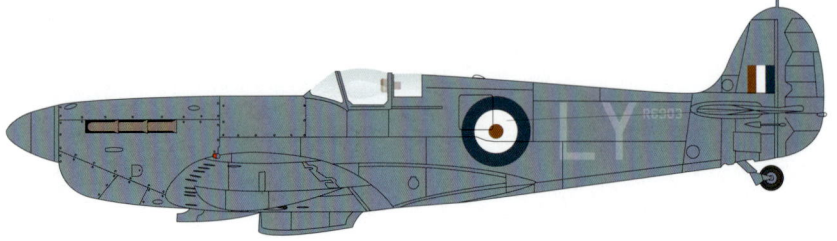

Spitfire PR Mk Id (Trop)
BR416 of No 2 PRU, based at Marble Arch, Libya, 1942

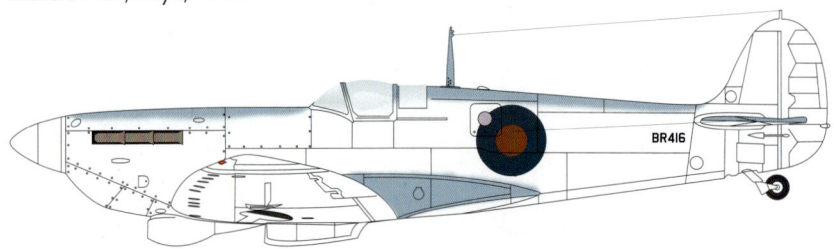

and a single Spitfire was converted to carry an oblique camera – possibly the first such fitting in the world – under each wing. Confusingly, it was designated the PR Mk Ie and even more confusingly, it was later upgraded to PR Mk V. The mark numbers of the Spitfire PR models gets even more confused now.

In March 1940, an interim before the Mk Id came off the line, more fuel was added to the Mk I fighter in fairings below the wings and this allowed the Photoreconnaissance Development Unit's Spitfire Mk If to reach Berlin, a round trip of four and a half hours. In 1941, these Spitfires were again upgraded to PR Mk IV standard.

By 1941, the urgent demand for fighters to protect the home base had receded but the need to provide overseas commands with adequate reconnaissance and intelligence gathering equipment remained and, if anything, grew as the conflict widened. Photo-reconnaissance was becoming

Spitfire PR Mk Id (Trop)
BP880, 'S' flown by Sergeant Ron Monkman of No 681 Squadron, RAF, based at Comilla, Bengal, 1944

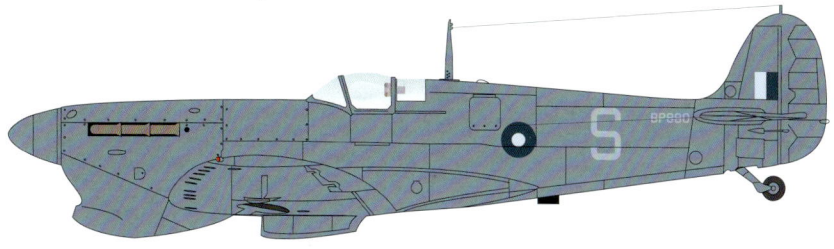

Spitfire PR Mk Ie
N3317/3, 'LY', flown by Flight Officer Alistair Taylor of PDU, based at RAF Heston, 7 July 1940

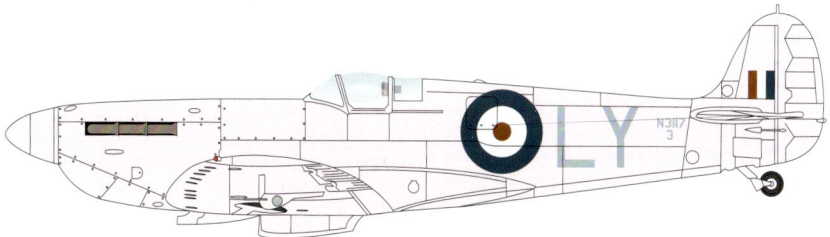

very important for bomb damage assessment as Bomber Command moved into gear. Range again was the driver for the PR Mk Id with its characteristic wing leading edge wing tanks – these bowser wings were developed at Hursley Park and fitted at Salisbury. With the extra wing tanks, the fuel capacity was now 218 Imp gal and a range of cameras could be carried. Supermarine worked with its suppliers to give the Royal Air Force a suite of camera installations.

At the same time, it became clear that low level reconnaissance was needed to make the oblique camera fitting worthwhile. Supermarine was asked to build a further 45 Mk Ia airframes but to modify them to carry the standard machine gun fit in self-defence and the fuselage fuel tank used in the PR Mk Ib. The result was the PR Mk Ig and, of course, it was upgraded and survivors became the PR Mk VII.

Spitfire PR Mk If
X4498, 'LY-E', flown by Squadron Leader R.P. Elliott of PDU, based at RAF Oakington, July 1941

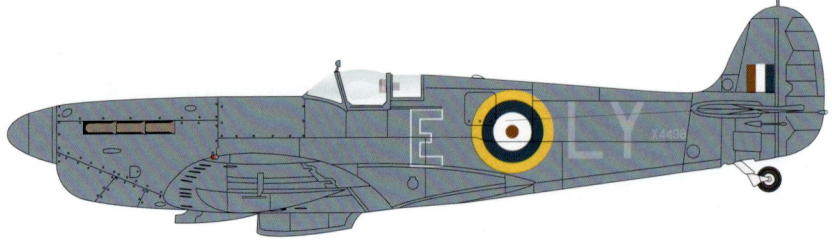

Spitfire PR Mk Ig
R7143 of 13 Photographic Survey Squadron, Royal Canadian Air Force based at Rockcliffe, Ontario, Canada, 1943

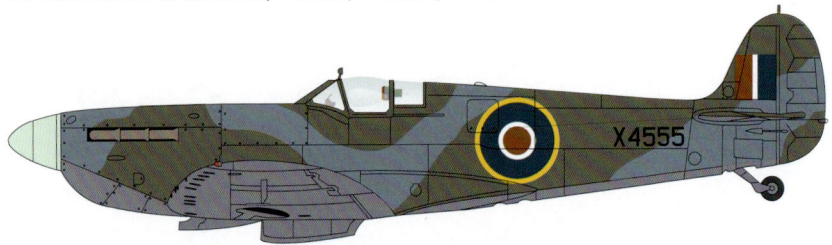

On 20 June 1941, this Spitfire PR Mk Ic was pictured at RAF Benson prior to operations.

Spitfire PR Mk IV
Serial unknown, of PRU, 1942

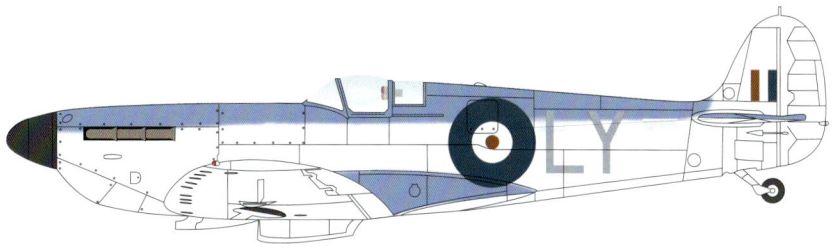

Spitfire PR Mk IV (Trop)
BP880, 'S/The Flying Scotsman' of No 681 Squadron, RAF, based at Chandina, India, February 1943

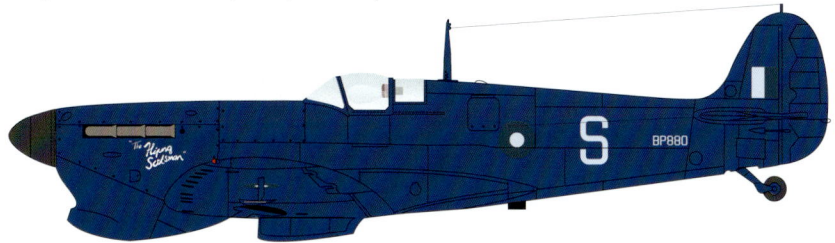

SPITFIRE EVOLUTION

OVERMATCHING

As Germany developed the design and power of the Bf 109, Fighter Command needed to match and, if possible, overmatch current Bf 109F and anticipated future models. In early 1941, the Spitfire still retained its agility advantage but was falling behind in combat speed at altitude – firepower was becoming an also issue.

To replace the Mk I and visually similar Mk II, Supermarine (by now at Hursley Park) was now working on the Mk III with the new Merlin XX powerplant which would necessitate a re-design of the forward fuselage. Production was now hitting the output required by the Ministry of Aircraft Production with lines at Castle Bromwich, Eastleigh and the dispersed factories in Salisbury and Trowbridge. The delay necessary to develop the Mk III was unacceptable.

The first Mk V was an interim development of the standard Mk I/II airframe with a new Merlin 45 engine so was easier to fabricate and required very little work on the production line, which allowed late production Mk IIs to be built as Mk Vs.

No 92 Squadron at Biggin Hill, in the thick of the cross-Channel fighting, was selected to be the first Mk V unit in February 1941 but pilots like Geoffrey Wellum found that the carburettor design still caused the engine to falter in negative G flight during dogfights.

Two initial variants were developed: Mk Va with eight machine guns (as favoured by Douglas Bader) and Vb with two 20 mm cannon and four

---

Spitfire Mk Va
W3185, 'DB', flown by Wing Commander Douglas Bader of the Tangmere Wing, RAF based at RAF Tangmere, 1941

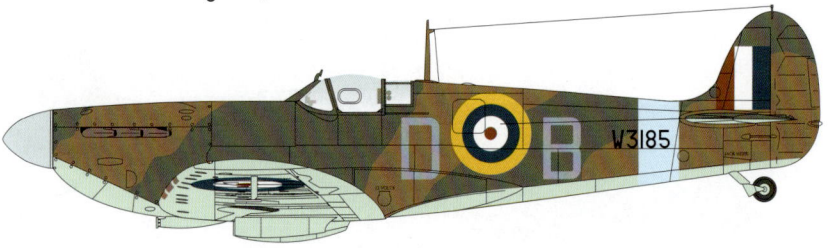

This Spitfire Mk Vb has been painted with the name Andover for the Hampshire town which raised £5,514 for the local Spitfire Fund. It survived the war.

Spitfire Mk Vb

BL292, 'YT.K' flown by Sergeant Vladimir Kopecek of No 65 (East India) Squadron, RAF based at RAF Debden, early 1942

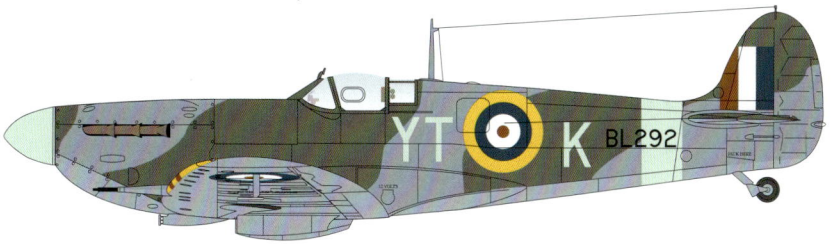

Spitfire Mk LF Vb

BL415, 'AZ.B' flown by Flight Lieutenant Walt 'Johnnie' Johnston of No 234 (Madras Presidency) Squadron, RAF based at RAF Deanland, 6 June 1944

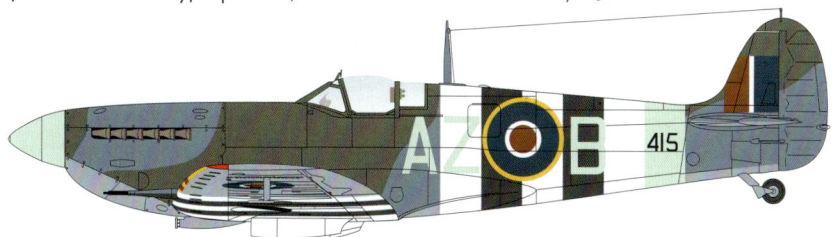

SPITFIRE EVOLUTION

machine guns. Later the power plants were optimised for low level combat (LF Mk V) with a Merlin 45M, 50M or later 55M to counter the Bf 109F's advantage below 12,000 ft; this meant that the standard Mk V was identified as Mk F V. In October, Supermarine created the 'c wing' into which could be fitted combinations of cannon and machine gun; it was designated the Mk Vc.

The Mk V was the first variant to carry bombs and 30 Imp Gal drop tanks to extend the range; these latter were later increased to 80 gal capacity as the engines developed more power which gave the Mk V almost twice the rate of climb of the first Mk I.

The Spitfire Mk V was sent to Malta and later North Africa and Australia. At home, Fighter Command's superiority over the Bf 109 would last only until September 1941 when the first Fw 190 fighters appeared over Occupied France and Belgium. It was time for the Spitfire to be further developed.

Spitfire Mk Vb (Trop)
ER874, 'AX.N/Cirecooks V' flown by Lieutenant Shalk Willem van der Merwe of No 1 Squadron, SAAF based at Goubrine, Tunisia, 17 April 1943

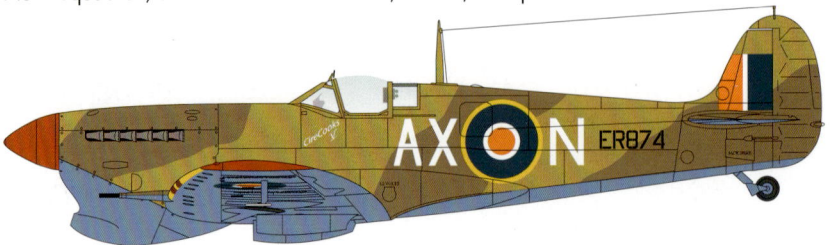

Spitfire Mk Vb (Trop)
ER622, 'WR.D' of No 40 Squadron, SAAF, based at Gabes, Tunisia, April 1943

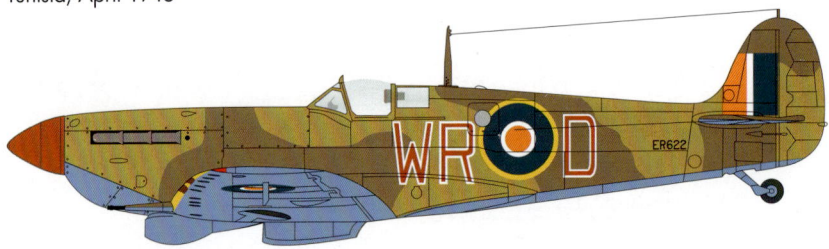

Another evolutionary point was the airscrew. Different propellers were fitted, according to where the Spitfire Mk V was built: Supermarine and Westland manufactured Mk Vb and Mk Vc used the 3- bladed de Havilland constant speed units, with narrow metal blades. Spitfire Mk Vb and Vc built at the Castle Bromwich Aircraft Factory were fitted with a wide-bladed metal Rotol constant speed propellers or, later, the broader, compressed wood blades known as *Jablo* blades. To distinguish between Rotol spinner and DH spinners: the former were longer and more pointed allowing better performance at altitude. Many Spitfire Mk Vb fighters were fitted with gun heater intensifier systems on the exhaust stacks which piped additional heated air into the gun bays. The recognition feature here is a short tubular intake on the front of the first stack and a narrow pipe led into the engine cowling from the rear exhaust.

Spitfire Mk Vc
AB216, 'DL.Z' flown by Squadron Leader Robert Oxspring of No 91 Squadron, RAF based at RAF Hawkinge, May 1942

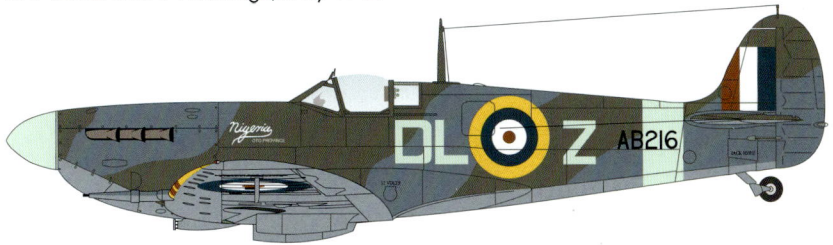

Spitfire Mk Vc (Trop)
BR323, 'S', flown by Sergeant George 'Buzz' Beurling of No 249 Squadron, RAF, based in Malta, July 1942

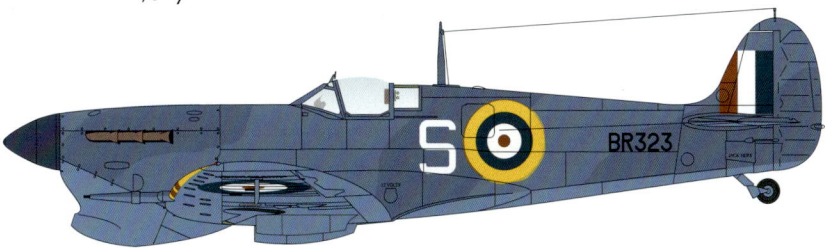

SPITFIRE MK VB FLOATPLANE

Not so much evolution as revolution. Using techniques and knowledge from the Schneider Trophy seaplanes, project director Arthur Shirvall worked with Supermarine and Folland Aircraft designers in 1940 during the Norway campaign to create a Spitfire Mk I but the conflict ended before the concept could be proved. On 12 October 1942, Folland received an order to fit new twin floats to a Mk Vb following Air Ministry interest in an island-hopping seaplane fighter for the Mediterranean and although three were completed and sent to Egypt, the plan was dropped. There was a Mk IX floatplane concept but it, too, was shelved.

Spitfire Mk Vb Floatplane
EP754, RAF, Great Bitter Lake, Egypt,
December 1943

THE SPITFIRE PRESSURISED

In a bid to engage high-flying German reconnaissance aircraft operating over Britain and over Egypt, the Air Ministry asked Supermarine if could provide a Spitfire " with a pressure cabin capable of maintaining a pressure differential of 1 lb per square inch at 40,000 feet." Joe Smith and the team at Hursley rose to the challenge and created 100 specially modified airframes.

The engineering challenges included enclosing the forward and rear cockpit bulkheads with specially cabling ducts through special rubber sealing grommets.

The cockpit door opening was covered with an alloy skin and the canopy was locked in place with four toggles and sealed with an inflatable rubber tube. It could be jettisoned by the pilot in an emergency but not routinely slid back.

As the *Luftwaffe* declined, there was no a need for armed high flying Spitfires and the Egypt-based Mk IV airframes were converted for photo-reconnaissance, serving between April and August 1943 with the nomenclature PR Mk IV.

In Britain, Fighter Command could find little use for the high flying Spitfire Mk IV (sometimes referred to as the HF Mk IV) after September 1943 and the variant was withdrawn from front line service and allocated to Training Command. The role of the High Altitude Interceptor was placed in the hands of Mk IX units, primarily based at RAF Northolt and these proved adequate on the rare times that German bombers appeared over Southern England.

Spitfire HF Mk VI
BS141, 'RY.E' of 313 (Czech) Squadron, RAF based at RAF Peterhead, June 1943

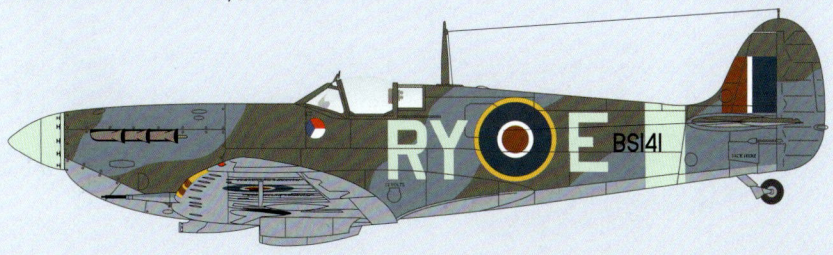

SPITFIRE EVOLUTION   27

HIGH FLYER

The Spitfire design evolved in 1941, coincidental with the re-organisation of the design and technical departments under Joe Smith and the move to Hursley Park. Almost the first priority was the evolving and then overriding need to bring together the Merlin 61 which, with a two-stage supercharger, would allow the ability to fight at altitude. That is where the *Luftwaffe* now had the advantage with the new Focke Wulf Fw 190 which was earning the nickname of 'butcher bird'.

The first of these re-designed Spitfires was created from the sole Mk III airframe and first flew on 27 September 1941. The design evolved into a pressurised high altitude fighter, the Mk VII, and the unpressurised Mk VIII.

Designed at Hursley Park with the specific role of high altitude aerial combat and flying in early 1942, the Mk VII was more advanced in concept than the Mk V, which it was to replace, and even the Mk IX. Both these variants were official 'stop gap' developments but would be built in greater quantities than any other marks.

The Spitfire's structural profile also evolved with Mk VII as, for the first time, the underwing intakes were symmetrical to improve the cooling provision, necessary with the new powerplant.

Capable of reaching 44,000 ft, the Mk VII high altitude variant brought together the Mk VI airframe and the two-stage Merlin 61, 64 or later 71 engines, giving at least 1660 hp at sea level. The use of the two-stage supercharger allowed this Spitfire to climb and still have 1300 hp available.

Spitfire Mk HF VII
MD172, 'NX.L' of No 133 Squadron,
RAF, RAF Harrowbeer, June 1944

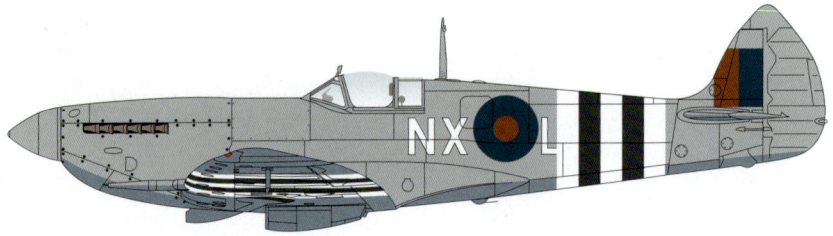

28 SPITFIRE EVOLUTION

The Merlin 71 gave the Mk VII more than 400 mph at altitudes greater than 40,000 ft altitude. The new engines also required a further lengthening of the fuselage and structural strengthening in the after fuselage to accommodate a retractable tail wheel. Causing 'recognition-confusion', some also had a pointed tail.

Fuselage modifications for pressurisation included a sliding cockpit hood, rather than the interim locked approach of the Mk VI – that would certainly have had high pilot approval ratings. So although the Mk VII was an evolutionary model, it still used features from the interim Mk VI. These features included the characteristic wing tip, which aided recognition, and were designed into the two wing types: the B wing with two Hispano cannon and four Browning machine guns or eight Browning guns of the 'universal wing' or C wing with combinations of cannon and machine guns. The former had a bowser wing from the Hursley drawing board and the craftsmen at Salisbury. The latter was redesigned by Alf Faddy and his team to make production easier and faster, and could carry heavier armament, including four cannon.

Only 140 were built because the Mk IX was found to be adequate for a diminishing *Luftwaffe* threat and the specialist high altitude role was phased out.

The unpressurised Mk VIII was also coming along and would be developed for sandy and tropical environments, fitting the Vokes Aero-Vee filter system to protect the Merlin engine. The standard C wing was fitted with either four Hispano 20 mm or two cannon and four machine guns. Later examples of the 1,658 Mk VIIIs even carried two 500 lb bombs

---

Spitfire Mk VIII
A58-528, 'CRC' flown by Wing Commander Clive 'Killer' Caldwell of No 80 Fighter Wing, RAAF, based at Morotai, Dutch East Indies, March 1945

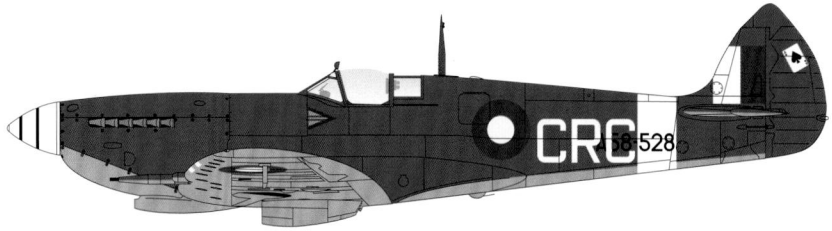

– they also had a cut down rear fuselage to give the fighter pilot a better view behind and a bubble canopy. These developments were so successful that they were adopted in late model Mk IXs on the Castle Bromwich production line and for the later Mk XVI.

Because of developing needs of Fighter Command and overseas units, these various roles and the engines available created a new mark designation system:

- F Mk VIII with the Merlin 61 (1560 hp) was the standard fighter
- LF Mk VIII fitted the Merlin 66 (1705 hp) was optimised for low altitude fighting
- HF Mk VIII was the Merlin 70 (1655 hp) was optimised for high altitude combat

It took eight months for the Mk VIII to see operational service after the first flight in November 1942. This variant did not see home service but went to Malta and then to Australia and South East Asia from 1943. In Burma, the Mk VIII was superior to the Kawasaki Ki 44, the standard fighter of the Japanese Imperial Army Air Force. The Royal Australia Air Force operated the Mk VIII in defence of Darwin and then in the ground attack role as Japanese forces were pushed back.

Perhaps because of the Mk VIII's operational service, predominantly in South East Asia Command, there are few examples which survived in Europe. This is despite having served in the Mediterranean theatre with both US and South African Air Force units.

Spitfire Mk VIII
JF472, ZX.J' flown by Squadron Leader Lance 'Wildcat' Wade of No 145 Squadron, RAF based at San Severo, Italy, 1943

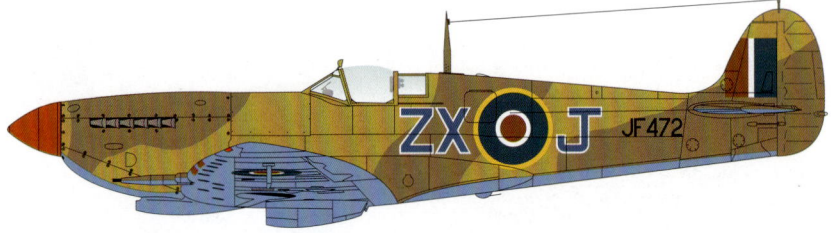

A SUPERB DOGFIGHTER

Following a short stint with an operational squadron, Captain Eric 'Winkle' Brown, then a Farnborough test pilot, described the Spitfire Mk IX as "an outstanding dogfighter" and an equal to the Focke Wulf Fw 190A.

Arguably Germany's greatest fighter aeroplane, the Fw 190 had surprised Fighter Command when it appeared in the summer of 1941 but it took until the autumn for a clear identification to be made. Yet again Supermarine and Rolls-Royce moved into revolutionary mode and developed a counter. In September 1941, the Spitfire Mk III prototype was fitted with a Merlin 60 engine, a development for high altitude versions of the Wellington bomber.

Because of pressure on Joe Smith's design team at Hursley Park, already

Spitfire Mk F IX
BF273 of Aeroplane and Armament Experimental Establishment, Boscombe Down, October 1942

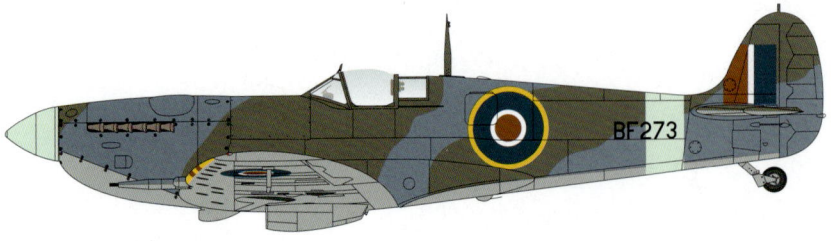

Spitfire Mk IXb
MK892, 'ZD.C' of No 222 Squadron, RAF based at RAF Coolham, June 1944

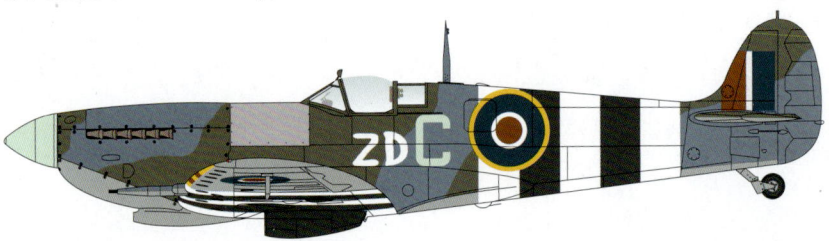

working on the Mk VII and Mk VIII, it was estimated that a newly designed Spitfire to counter the Fw 190 might take until 1943. Fighter Command could not wait, so evolution played its hand again and some Mk Vc airframes (retaining the double cannon blisters) were modified to take the new Merlin.

Supermarine delivered a modified Mk Vc to the Air Fighting Development Unit in April 1942 and the 'quantum leap' in performance was immediately noticeable especially at altitude and in a battle climb. The Ministry of Aircraft Production moved the Mk IX production line to Castle Bromwich Aircraft Factory in June 1943 and the design was progressively improved with more powerful Merlin 66 engines, new radiators and the Bendix-Stromberg injection carburettor, replacing the earlier Skinners' Union float carburettor which had been causing alarming performance glitches through fuel starvation since the Battle of Britain.

Spitfire Mk IXc
MJ586, 'LO.D' flown by Sous Lieutenant P.H. Clostermann of No 602 Squadron, RAF, based at B11, Longues, France, July 1944

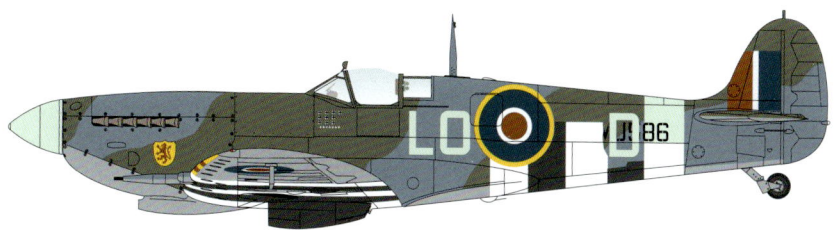

Spitfire Mk IXe
MK392, 'JE.J' flown by Wing Commander J.E. 'Johnnie' Johnson, Officer Commanding 144 Wing, RAF based at RAF Ford, June 1944

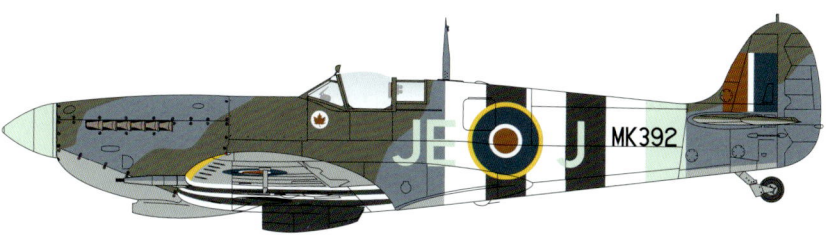

As the mainstay of Fighter Command from 1942 to 1945, the Mk IX had its wing armament developed in the light of dogfighting experience. Working with the Air Ministry, Supermarine evolved the E-wing configuration of two 20 mm cannon and two 0.50 cal (12.7 mm) machine guns in each wing. A rounded tail, as originally designed for the Mk I/II was found on most Mk IX production models but towards the end of 1944, the more pointed tail of the Mk VII was evolved into the Mk IX design.

Britain would start to develop specialist types from late 1943, allowing two distinct but outwardly similar versions of the Spitfire Mk IX to appear from early 1944. The LF Mk IX was created for low level air fighting with the Merlin 66 powerplant and the HF Mk IX featured the Merlin 70 as the high altitude variant. At the same time, advances in gun sights were made together with the provision of slipper and jettisonable drop tanks. The Shenstone wing

Spitfire LF Mk IXe
MK356, '5J.K' as flown by Squadron Leader Johnny Plagis of
No 126 Squadron, June 1944

Spitfire Mk IX
TA805, FX.M' as operated by No 234 (Madras Presidency)
Squadron, June 1944. Now named 'Spirit of Kent'

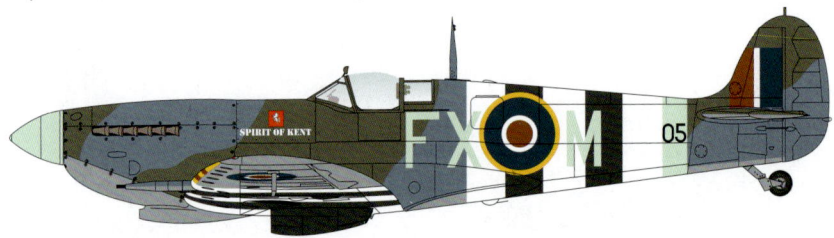

design was found to be capable of development to improve weight carriage without damaging performance or intervals between inspections. Some late model Mk IX fighters were fitted with the Packard Merlin 266 engine and they can be recognised by the distinctive bulged cowling to incorporate the integral header tank.

With its ease of production and general good all-round performance, the Spitfire Mk IX was retained in production and upgraded. From late 1944, the rear fuselage was cut down and a bubble canopy fitted for better visibility in a dogfight. This had been tried and tested on the Mk VIII and found to improve situational awareness and therefore survivability. Fuel management and stability were improved by changing the tank capacities – the lower forward fuselage tank was increased to 47 Imp gals, compensated by the rear tanks decrease to 66 Imp gals.

Spitfire Mk FR IXc
MK915, 'V' of No 16 Squadron, No 34 (Reconnaisance) Wing, RAF based at A12 Balleroy, France, September 1944

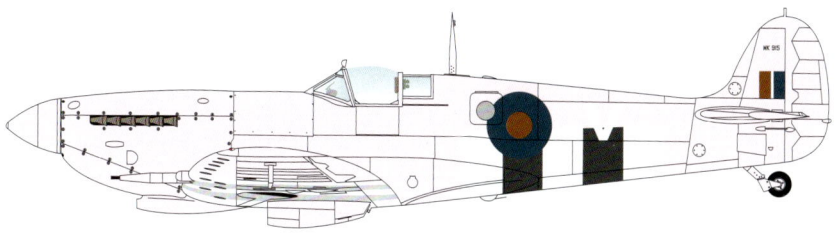

Spitfire Mk IX
MK732 (PH-OUQ) was Castle Bromwich-built and after service with No 485 (NZ) Squadron, she was sold to the Royal Netherlands Air Force in 1948

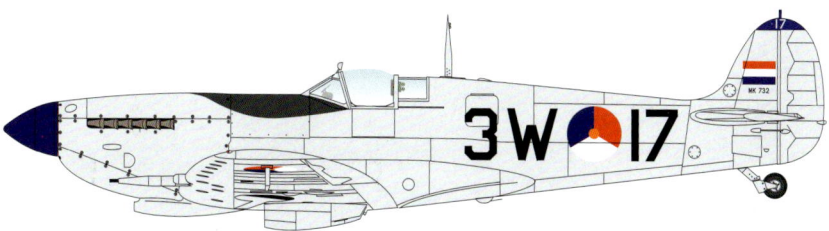

A wing

The standard, original configuration of eight Browning rifle calibre machine guns as originally conceived by the Air Ministry in 1936.

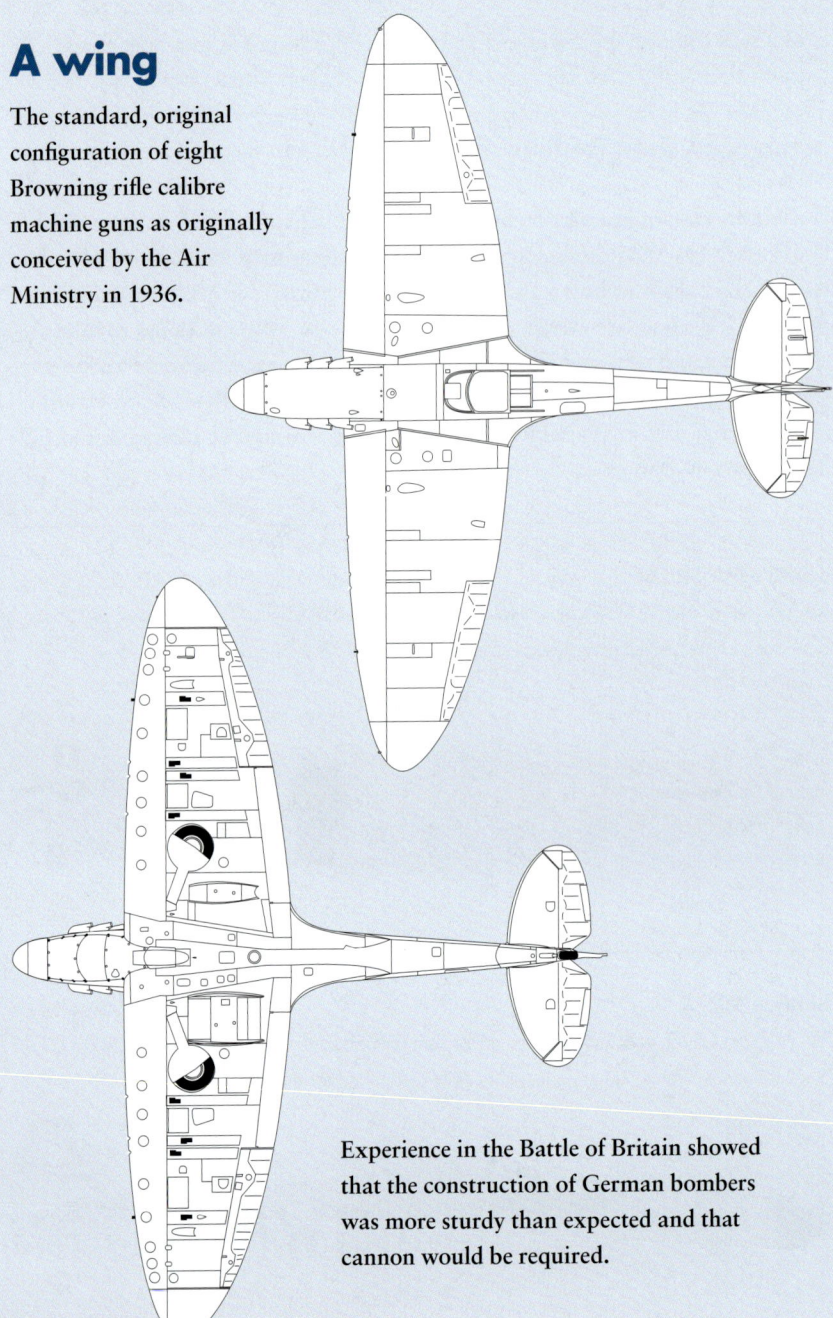

Experience in the Battle of Britain showed that the construction of German bombers was more sturdy than expected and that cannon would be required.

B wing

The first attempts to fit cannon into the slender Shenstone wing design failed and an internal re-design by the Faddy team was needed.

The result was the B Wing which included blisters for the drum-fed Hispano Mk II weapons. These could now operate even when the fighter pulled significant G. A by-product was the increase of Browning machine gun ammunition by 20%.

SPITFIRE EVOLUTION

C wing

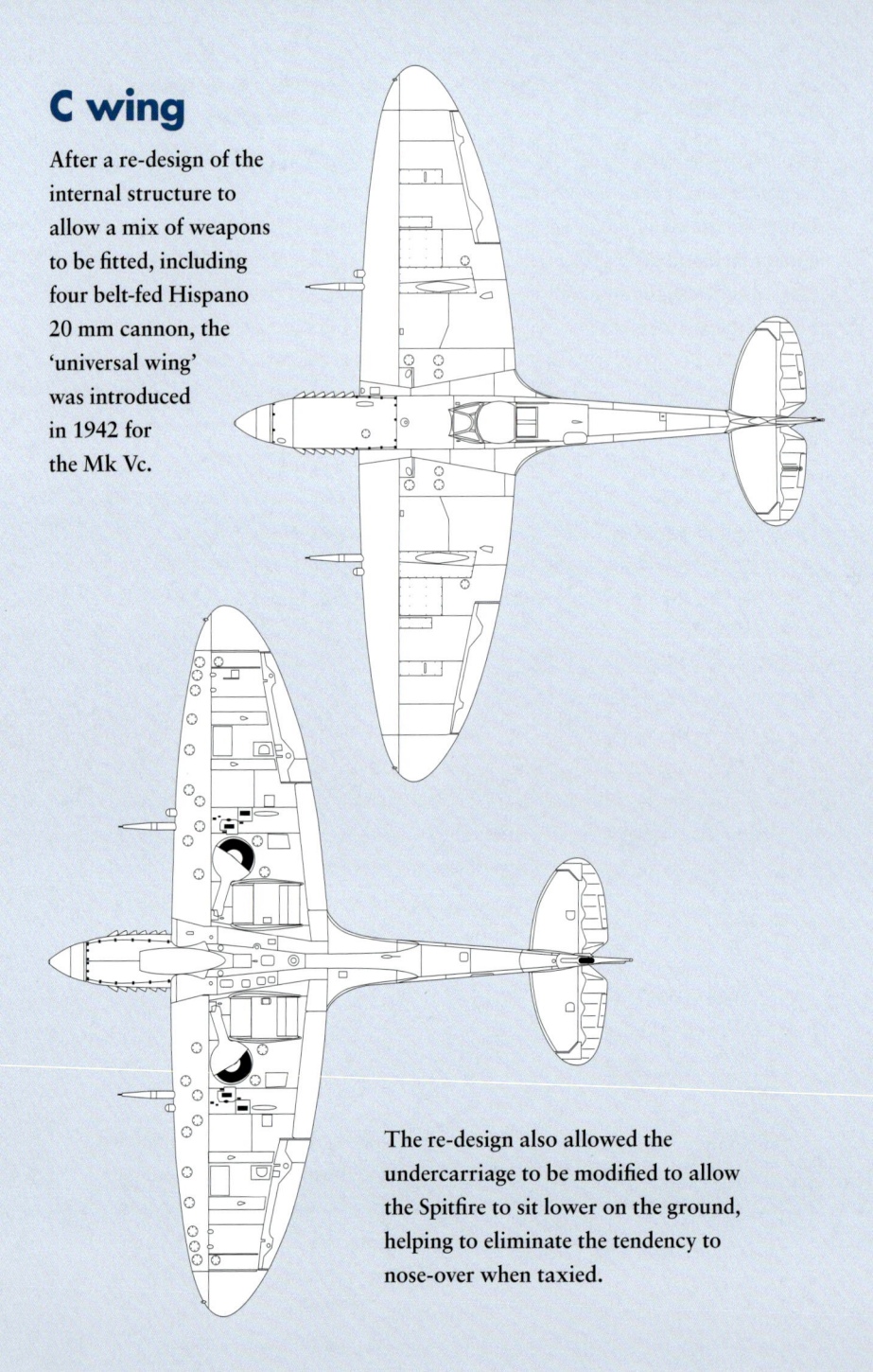

After a re-design of the internal structure to allow a mix of weapons to be fitted, including four belt-fed Hispano 20 mm cannon, the 'universal wing' was introduced in 1942 for the Mk Vc.

The re-design also allowed the undercarriage to be modified to allow the Spitfire to sit lower on the ground, helping to eliminate the tendency to nose-over when taxied.

D wing

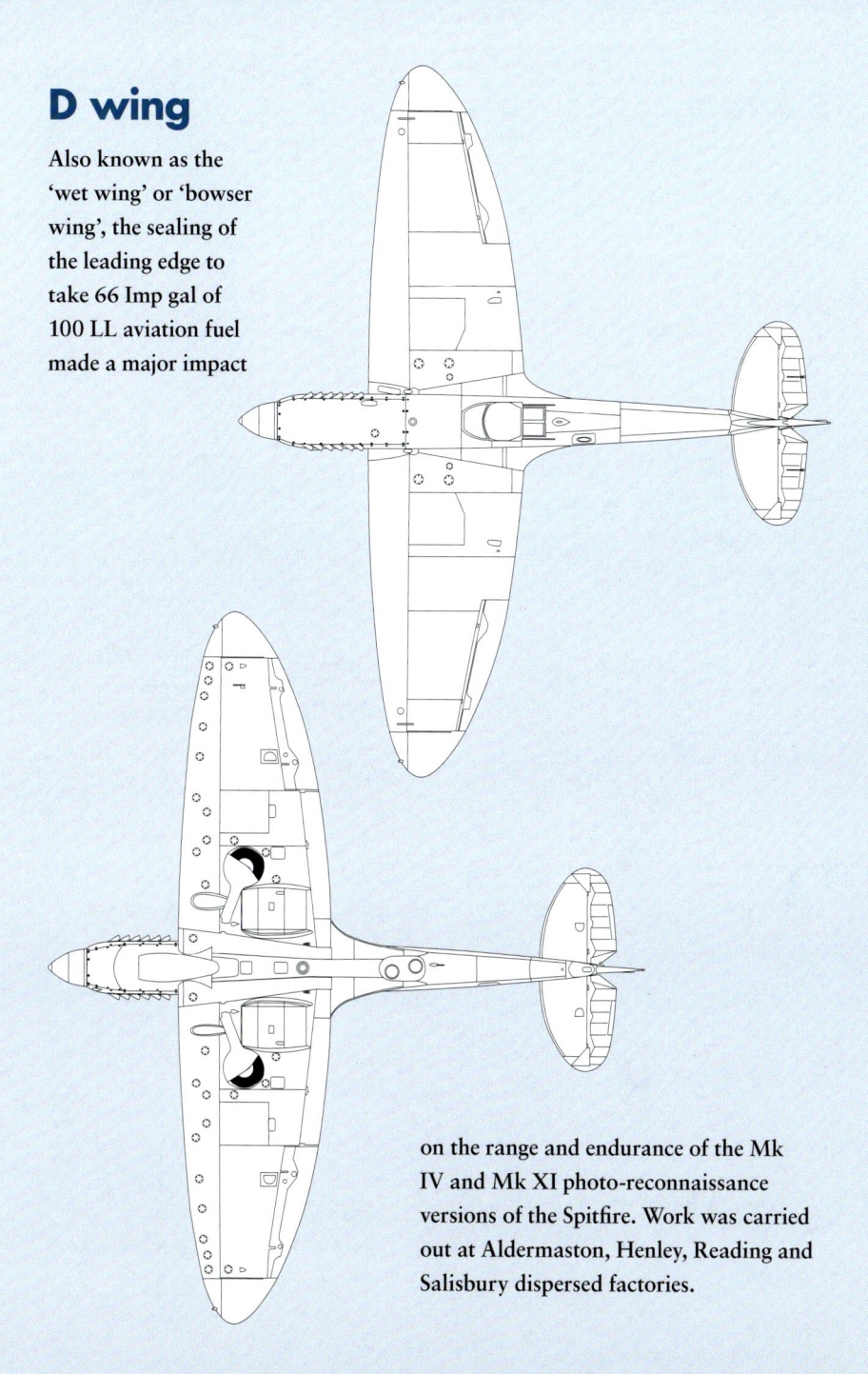

Also known as the 'wet wing' or 'bowser wing', the sealing of the leading edge to take 66 Imp gal of 100 LL aviation fuel made a major impact on the range and endurance of the Mk IV and Mk XI photo-reconnaissance versions of the Spitfire. Work was carried out at Aldermaston, Henley, Reading and Salisbury dispersed factories.

SPITFIRE EVOLUTION

E wing

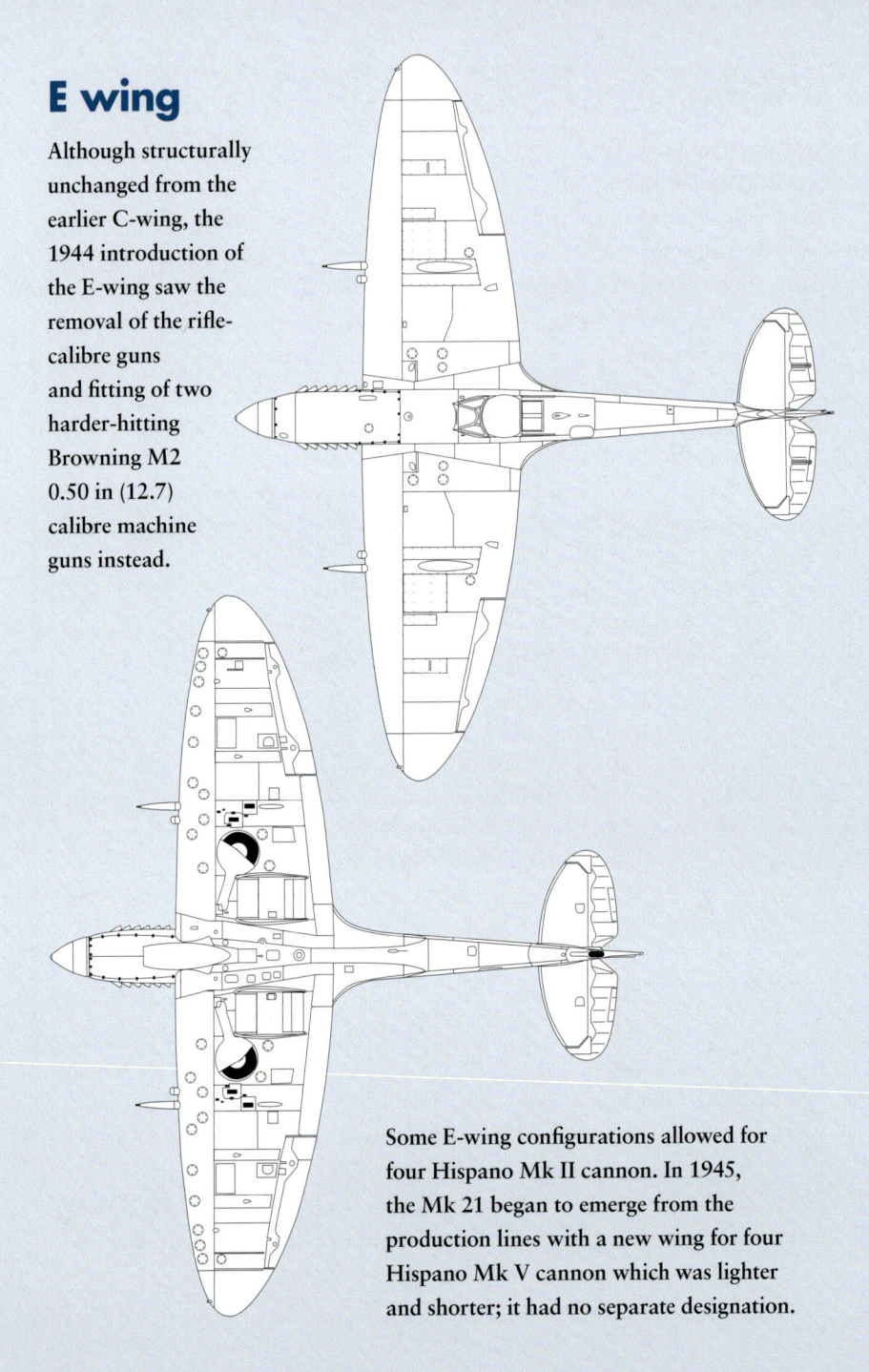

Although structurally unchanged from the earlier C-wing, the 1944 introduction of the E-wing saw the removal of the rifle-calibre guns and fitting of two harder-hitting Browning M2 0.50 in (12.7) calibre machine guns instead.

Some E-wing configurations allowed for four Hispano Mk II cannon. In 1945, the Mk 21 began to emerge from the production lines with a new wing for four Hispano Mk V cannon which was lighter and shorter; it had no separate designation.

Clipped wing

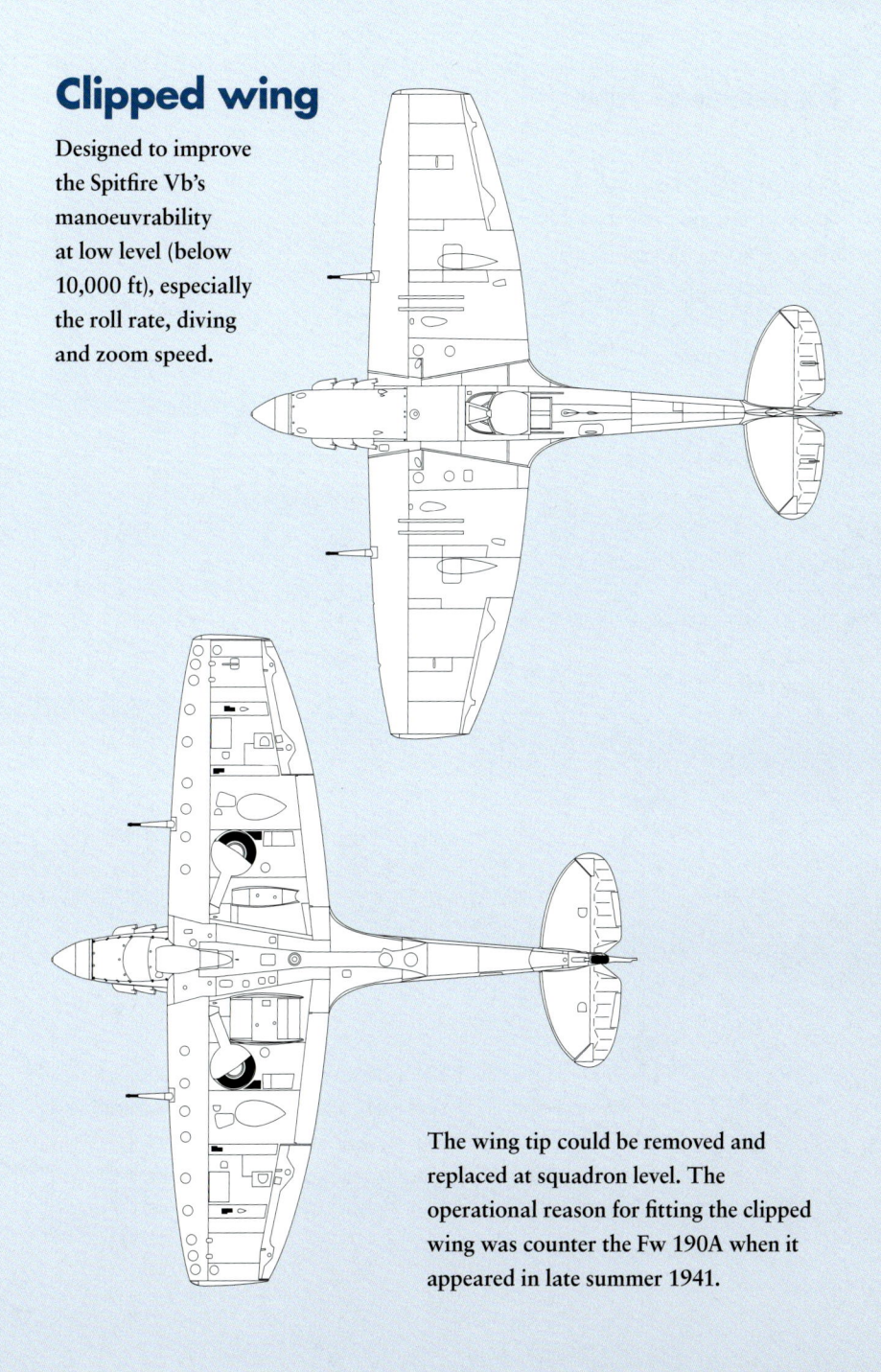

Designed to improve the Spitfire Vb's manoeuvrability at low level (below 10,000 ft), especially the roll rate, diving and zoom speed.

The wing tip could be removed and replaced at squadron level. The operational reason for fitting the clipped wing was counter the Fw 190A when it appeared in late summer 1941.

SPITFIRE EVOLUTION

Extended tips

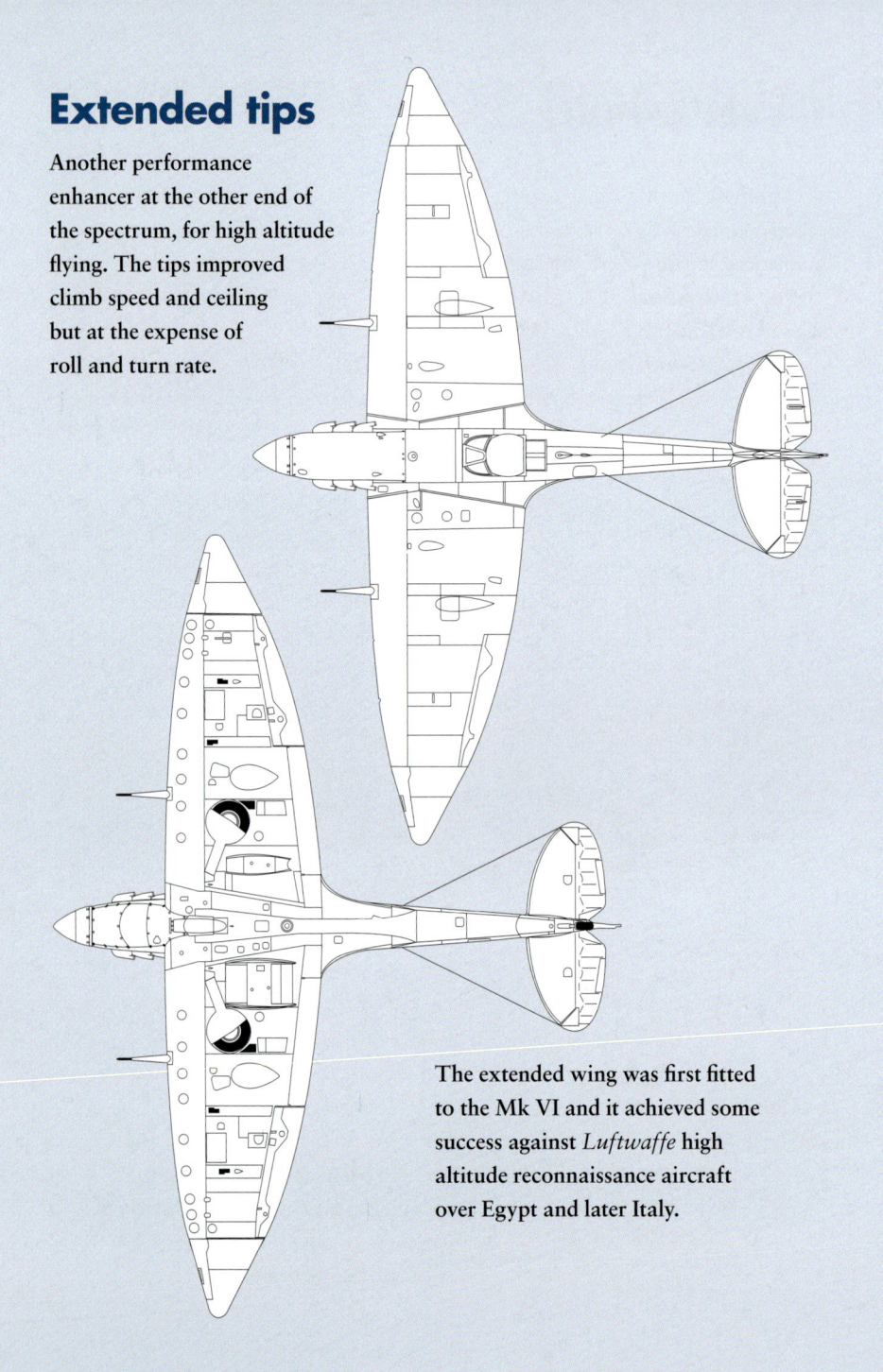

Another performance enhancer at the other end of the spectrum, for high altitude flying. The tips improved climb speed and ceiling but at the expense of roll and turn rate.

The extended wing was first fitted to the Mk VI and it achieved some success against *Luftwaffe* high altitude reconnaissance aircraft over Egypt and later Italy.

THE TWO-SEAT TRAINERS

In 1944, with an eye to the future export market for the Spitfire, Vickers bought back a Spitfire airframe from the Ministry of Aircraft Production and sent it to High Post airfield, north of Salisbury. Using drawings prepared at Hursley Park, a small team prepared to evolve the single-seater into a two-seat trainer. Vickers planned to create 48 Spitfire Mk TR 8s but in the end only one was built – it is still airworthy today.

In 1942-43, 140 Spitfire Mk Vb was delivered to the Soviet Frontal Aviation and later a large number of Mk IXs were provided under lend-lease for the PVO (air defence organisation). Some of these airframes were crudely modified in 1945 by No 1 Aircraft Depot at Leningrad and acted as lead-in trainer for

---

Spitfire Mk T VIII

With the export market in mind, this Mk T VIIIc was fitted with a large bubble canopy for the instructor in a second cockpit. MT818 is today owned by Paul Andrews and operated in Britain.

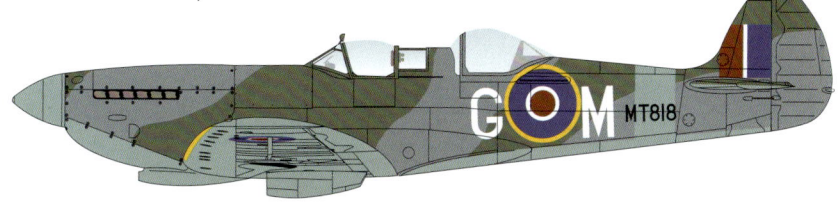

Spitfire Mk T9

Modified from a Mk IX with a credible war record, this two-seat trainer was operated by the Irish Army Air Corps before being bought by the Grace family. It has a lower profile canopy, known as a Grace Hood after its designer, the late Nick Gray.

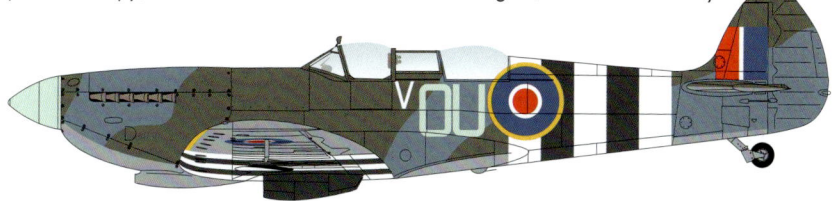

Soviet pilots who had found the earlier Spitfire challenging. It is believed that this two-seat, dual-control variant was known as the Spitfire IX, UTI, the dual control trainer abbreviation.

In 1946, Supermarine revived the training option for the Spitfire as surplus singe-seaters were being offered by the British Government to air forces reforming or developing. The Mk IX was chosen as the airframe and 20 were modified at Eastleigh and Chilbolton. The largest customer was India (10), followed by Ireland (six), the Netherlands (three) and a single example for Egypt.

With advances in engineering and an evolving regulatory environment, a small number of Spitfire Mk IXs were taken on by commercial companies for conversion. A growing market for Spitfire Experiences means more are likely to be converted or re-built to Mk TR 9 standards in the future.

Spitfire Mk TR 9

Another Mk IX conversion, the Boultbee Spitfire was originally built at Castle Bromwich as a single seater but converted in Britain by Classic Aero Engineering at Thruxton. To maintain the C of G, the front cockpit was moved forward 18 inches.

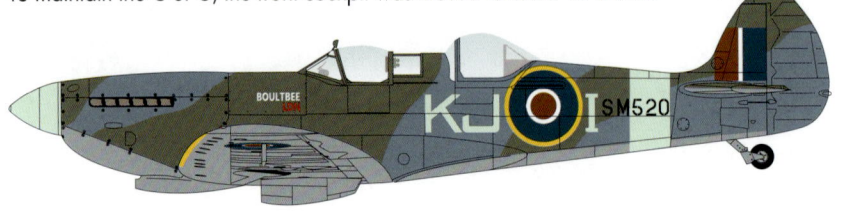

Spitfire Mk T 9

Built as a single-seat Spitfire Mk IX and was flown by No 441 Squadron of the Royal Canadian Air Force. Since being modified into a two-seat trainer, she has also been used for experience flights from Goodwood and Biggin Hill.

With the export market in mind, this Mk T VIIIc was fitted with a large bubble canopy for the instructor in a second cockpit. MT818 is today owned by Paul Andrews and operated in Britain.

Spitfire Mk T9 (Modified)
Featuring the streamlined Grace-style second hood, this Spitfire Mk IX was to serve with the Royal Air Force, Italian Air Force and Israel Defence Force. It is now based in Wales and known as the Red Dragon Spitfire

Spitfire Mk IXT
Built as a Mk IX fighter and flown by No 33 Squadron, this Spitfire was then old to Vickers and converted to a two-seater for the Irish Army Air Corps. Since 2003, she has been flown in various guises from Duxford.

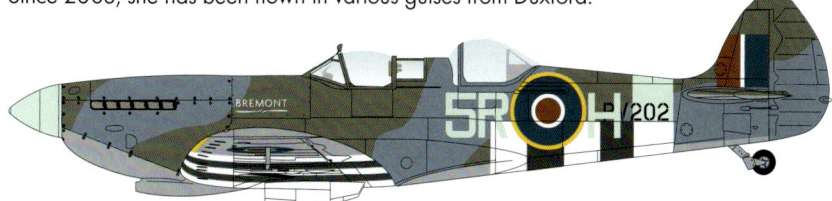

SPITFIRE EVOLUTION   **45**

FASTER SPY IN THE SKY

Early Spitfire PR models were successful in evading the enemy and brought back superb pictures across Occupied Europe and Germany. But by 1942, there was a need to improve and evolve the capabilities.

In late 1942, three Mk IX airframes were taken from the Castle Bromwich line and fitted with vertical cameras for No 541 Squadron at RAF Benson, where they arrive in November. The Royal Air Force was impressed and another 15 airframes were sent to Worthy Down for development into an evolutionary design with a larger oil tank – always a limiting factor for Merlin-powered aircraft – and new canopy and windscreen arrangement to aid the pilot in the mission.

SPITFIRE PR MK X

Just 16 of these Merlin-engined Spitfire Mk VIIs were produced for high altitude photo-reconnaissance by No 541 and later No 542 Squadrons RAF Benson and re-designated Mk X. The basic design was to take the Mk VII airframe (which could be pressurised) and fit the Merlin 64 (and later the Merlin 71) engine and a larger oil tank for extended range operations. Other modifications included a retractable undercarriage and the Lobelle sliding canopy. Using the standard D Wing and a variety of cameras, these Spitfires had bowser tanks in the leading edges and at least one was later fitted with wing extensions. The advent of the Griffon and re-design of the Spitfire airframe by Joe Smith's team evolved into the PR Mk XIX.

Spitfire PR Mk X
Painted with 'camoutint pink', SR396 of No 541 (PR) Squadron, RAF based at RAF Benson, January 1944

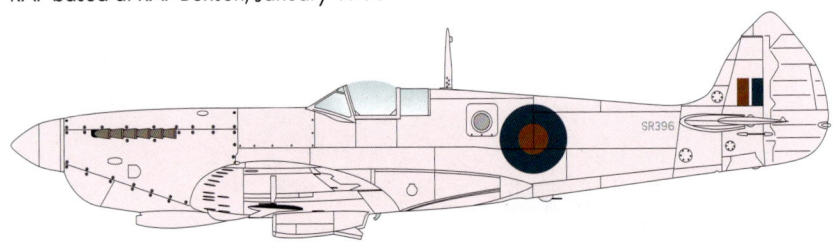

SPITFIRE PR MK XI

The non-pressurised version of the Mk X with a Merlin 61 (or 63 or 70 engine) and Vokes Aero Vee dust filter equipment was fitted at Aldermaston to the Mk VII airframe with a large oil tank and bowser wings. These were allocated to tactical reconnaissance operations so again modifications were made to the fuselage to allow oblique and vertical cameras to be carried, the latter in the rear fuselage for the first time. Also fitted with the same non-jettisonable slipper tanks as the Mk IX fighter, 471 Mk XIs were rolled out and test flown between November 1942 and April 1944. It was replaced by the PR Mk XIX in December 1944. The developments of camera and film technology in the Second World War, plus the evolving skills in interpretation made Britain the world leader in both the art and the science. It retains that capability today.

Spitfire PR Mk XI
This Aldermaston-built Spitfire completed 40 operational missions over enemy territory with No 16 Squadron before being sold to the Royal Netherlands Air Force. After restoration by Nick Grace, she is now displayed by Peter Teichman.

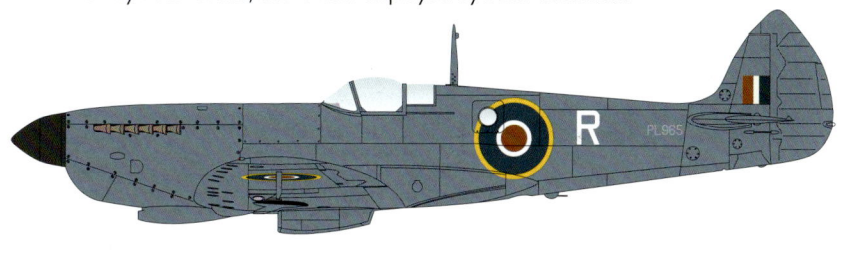

Spitfire PR Mk XI
This was a one-off private venture for aerial survey in Argentina in 1947, with the civilian registration LV-NMZ; it also illustrates the less-than desirable slipper tank under the cockpit.

ULTIMATE MERLIN

When Henry Ford refused to contribute the British war effort in the days before Pearl Harbor, the British Purchasing Commission, part of the Ministry of Supply, turned to the Packard Motor Car Company to place an order to produce Merlin engines. Packard offered excellent terms and had an first class engineering record which impressed Rolls-Royce and so the deal was done in September 1940 – US$ 130 millions' worth of engines.

By August 1941, the first Packard Merlin was running. It was known as the Merlin 28 (also known as the Merlin XX) with a single-stage, two-speed Farman supercharger and it was installed in the Lancaster and then the P-40F but it would be another year before Supermarine took a look at it for the Mk IX.

The Packard Merlin was impressive. It had been modified with silver-lead crankshaft bearings which withstood wear better and the crankshaft itself used a Pontiac indium-plated process which again improved performance and service life. Many of the Merlin engines flying in warbirds today were originally a Packard Merlin.

With Stanley Hooker at Rolls-Royce supervising, the Packard Merlin 266 was developed for a developed version of the Spitfire Mk IX, the Mk XVI – the ultimate Merlin Spitfire. The Merlin 266 installation can usually be recognised by a bulged upper cowling to fit the intercooler.

In evolutionary terms, the Mk XVI, of which 1,054 were built, showed the influence of the Americans – not just the Packard-built Merlin but also

---

Spitfire LF Mk XVIe
SL727 'HT.L' of No 601 (County of London) Squadron,
RAF, based at RAF North Weald, late 1949

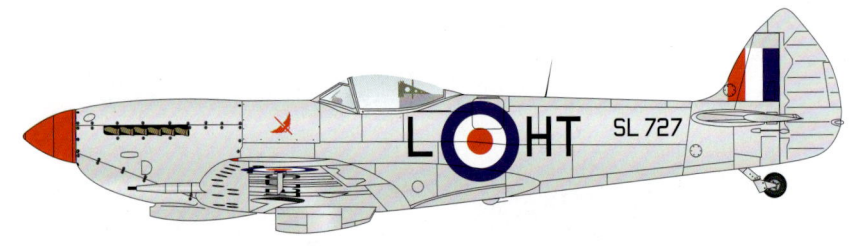

Spitfire Mk XVI

Now flown regularly in Scandinavia, this Mk XVI was built with tear drop canopy and cut down rear fuselage at Castle Bromwich. She was delivered to No 604 Squadron in March 1947 and later used for training at RAF Halton.
It was restored to flying by historic Flying Ltd by 2007.

Spitfire Mk XVIe

A later Mk XVI with a standard high back fuselage and marked for the gallant Czech pilots who flew with the Royal Air Force. Like most Mk XVIs, TE184 was built at Castle Bromwich in 1945 and powered by the Packard Merlin 266.

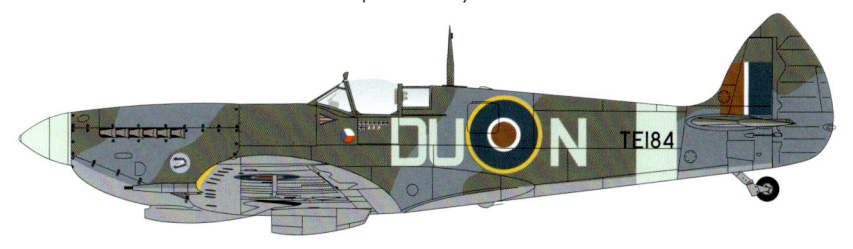

exclusive provision of the E Wing with the Browning M2 0.50 cal (12.7 mm) heavy machine guns and two Hispano Mk II cannon – or the machine guns removed and four cannon instead.

The overall shape was the same as the Mk IX but the development of the 'teardrop' canopy and cut-down rear fuselage, so important for air-fighting, was built in on the Castle Bromwich production line for the late model Mk XVI. Like the Mk IX, it had a Rotol four-bladed airscrew with pointed spinner. In fact, all Mk XVIs were built as LF marks and optimised for low altitude operations. To extend the range, tanks were fitted in rear fuselage for 75 Imp gal for conventional fuselage and 66 Imp gal for the cut-down version.

SPITFIRE EVOLUTION **49**

ENTER THE GRIFFON

By 1941, it was clear that the Rolls-Royce Merlin was coming to the end of its evolutionary process for the Spitfire. In 1938, the Fleet Air Arm, now under Admiralty control, requested a new engine for a range of naval fighters and strike aircraft including the Fairey Firefly. In November 1939, Rolls-Royce ran the new engine, called Griffon, in the continued homage to birds of prey. The Air Ministry was not slow to see its potential and neither was Supermarine.

So powerplant evolution was keeping pace with airframe evolution. Working closely together as they had for two decades, Rolls-Royce and Supermarine produced a new powerplant and airframe combination – the Spitfire Mk XII.

Nearly a metre longer than the Merlin-powered Spitfire Mk Vc and Mk VIII airframes which were initially used, the Mk XII was optimised to engage the *Luftwaffe*'s Focke Wulf Fw 190 at low level. To fit the larger and different Griffon engine, the Mk XII features two characteristic bulges above the exhaust ports. A retractable tail wheel was fitted to late models and these became standard on subsequent Spitfires.

To prove its capability, prior to service entry, Supermarine's Chief Test Pilot, Jeffrey Quill tasked the then Lieutenant Eric Brown with flying the length of Britain at low level and to report on the performance of the still secret aeroplane. Eric was delighted with the low level performance of 350 mph and finally touched down at Chattis Hill 'exhilarated'.

One of the Nation's premier fighter squadrons, No 41 was selected to pioneer the service entry and to emphasise the technological advantage.

Spitfire Mk XII
MB882, 'EB-B' flown by Flight Lieutenant Don Smith RAAF,
RAF based at RAF West Malling, 12 April 1944

Spitfire F Mk XIVc

This particular Mk XIV shows the high back fuselage and should be compared to NH869 below. RN135 flown by Squadron Leader James 'Ginger' Lacey of No 17 Squadron, RAF, based at Miho, Japan, May 1946

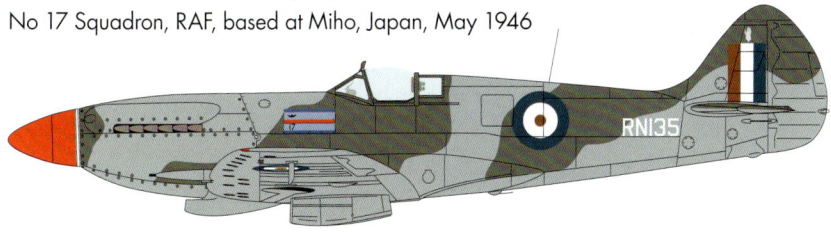

Spitfire FR Mk XIVe

A later production Mk XIV with bubble canopy and low back fuselage, NH869, 'H' of No 28 Squadron, RAF, based at Kuala Lumpur, 1946

The Air Ministry made pictures public, some of which were the first ones of a Spitfire released in colour. Only 100 Mk XII were built and have characteristic design elements including a pointed tail and wing armament of two 20 mm cannon and four 0.303 in Browning guns.

The improved Rolls-Royce Griffon engine was set to transform the Spitfire's performance as Supermarine developed the Mk VIII airframe, adding the new tail section to provide stability for the 2050 hp engine's torque. The Mk XIV evolved into a worthy successor of the Battle of Britain 'babies'. It looks like a different aeroplane and had been re-designed at Hursley to reflect new developments.

Air Transport Auxiliary pilot Joy Lofthouse recalls her first Griffon powered Spitfire flight from Eastleigh and even though the experienced ferry pilot was used to the Fairey Barracuda and other powerful aeroplanes, nothing prepared her for the swing of the Mk XIV on take-off or the raw power in the climb.

XVIII REDESIGN

Joe Smith's team had adapted the Griffon engine into the Spitfire Mk VIII airframe to create the Mk XIV but Supermarine now had the opportunity to move from evolution to revolution by going back to the drawing board.

Experience had shown that extra fuel was useful with the frequently thirsty Griffon 65. To achieve a greater fuel load would require a new wing with a stronger structure to carry the weight and to maintain integrity. Pilot experience had also shown that small refinements in the cockpit would make a great difference to flying and fighting the Spitfire, especially with the teardrop canopy.

The work on the Mk XVIII design and the need to produce existing variants in a less extreme warfighting environment meant that this mark of Spitfire missed the Second World War. In fact, the initial operating unit, No 60 Squadron at RAF Seletar (Singapore) would not receive its Mk XVIIIs until January 1947, almost a year after production had ended. This unit flew the last operational Spitfire sortie in the Royal Air Force on 1 January 1951.

The Indian Air Force acquired 20 Mk XVIII fighters in 1947 and they saw service over Kashmir in 1948. The Mk XVIII would also see active service in the Middle East when British, Egyptian and Israeli forces clashed during the War of Independence 1948-49; on 7 January 1949, Israel Defence Force Spitfire Mk IX fighters engaged and shot down three unarmed Mk XVIIIs of No 208 Squadron.

Two variants were delivered to the Royal Air Force; the F Mk XVIII with the standard E Wing and the FR Mk XVIII which was fitted with an oblique angle camera. The total production run was 300.

Spitfire FR Mk XVIe
TZ203 'J' of No 208 Squadron, RAF, based at Fayid, Egypt, 1949

Spitfire FR Mk XVIIIe

Showing the sleek lines of the Mk XVIII as the Spitfire would have appeared in 1950 when serving with No 28 Squadron in Hong Kong. This example is owned by Spitfire Ltd and is operated from Humberside.

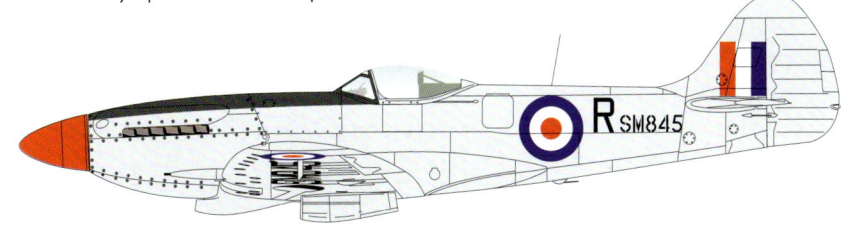

Spitfire FR Mk XVIIIe

Originally delivered to the Indian Air Force and rescued from a scrap yard in 1977. It was first restored in the USA, then improved at Historic Flying Ltd at Duxford and is now in Germany as part of the Meier Motors collection.

SPITFIRE EVOLUTION

LAST ACT

In fuel capacity terms alone, the Spitfire Mk XIX showed how the simple design for an eight-gun fighter had progressed in the 10 years from 1934. The Mk XIX, after the Spitfire had evolved through 90 modifications, could carry 256 Imp gal or 350% more fuel than the Mk I lifted when it entered service in August 1938.

This incarnation married the Griffon engine of the Mk XIV with many of the features of the Mk XI, including the wings, and, later, the pressurised cabin of the Mk X. The design still relied on a complex, streamlined, semi-monocoque duralumin fuselage with a large number of compound curves built up from a skeleton of 19 frames.

Many of the 225 built operated for up to 10 years with the Royal Air Force, rating the Mk 19 as the most successful of the photo-reconnaissance variants. Its development owes much to the evolution of the design from the Mk I in equipment terms and the development of the structure in terms of performance. Even a decade after production started at Wolston, the design still required partially the skills of a craftsman rather than production line worker.

The Mk XIX entered service in May 1944 and shared the same Pilot's Notes as the Mk XIV indicating the commonality in many areas, especially those related to flight performance. This would have made conversion training easier.

Although the XIX served in the front line until April 1954, by which time

---

Spitfire PR Mk XIX
PS890 (F-AZJS) represents No 152 (Panther) squadron, South East Asia Command. It is now based in France but had previously served with the Royal Thai Air Force.

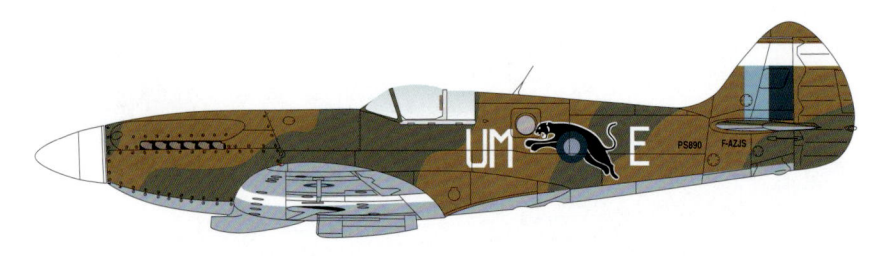

the designation had become Mk 19, it was robust enough for one last series of operational 'jet age' sorties for the Royal Air Force. In 1963, one of those allocated to the Battle of Britain Memorial Flight was used for the evaluation of dissimilar air combat techniques with a Fighter Command Lightning during the Borneo crisis when the Indonesian Air Force operated Mustangs. Unless the Lightning made a kill on the first pass, the Spitfire could out-manoeuvre it, proving the agility and robustness of the Joe Smith legacy.

Spitfire PR Mk XIX
The best known Mk XIX on the display circuit is G-RRGN (PS853) owned by Rolls-Royce Heritage which was built at Southampton and test flown from Eastleigh in 1944. This aeroplane was used extensively to identify V-weapon sites in Europe, using the vertically-mounted and oblique cameras. She flew nine sorties with No 541 Squadron based at RAF Benson. On leaving Royal Air Force service, she joined the Battle of Britain Memorial Flight, display flying until 1995 when she was purchased by Rolls-Royce. Her registration signifies the Griffon engine and she is generally known as the 'Rolls-Royce Spitfire'.

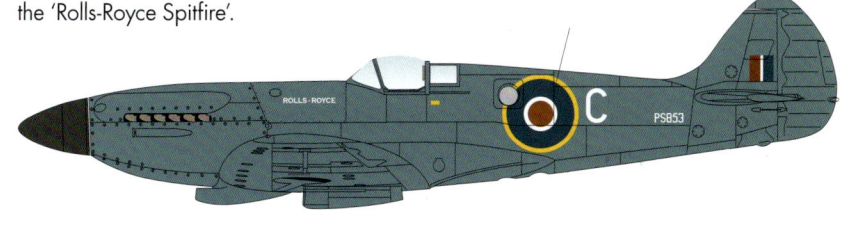

Spitfire PR Mk 19
PS852, No 81 Squadron, RAF Tengah (Singapore) on detachment to RAF Sek Kong (Hong Kong) for high altitude reconnaissance over Mainland China. It flew the last operational Spitfire flight on 1 April 1954. This is Spitfire is part of the BBMF.

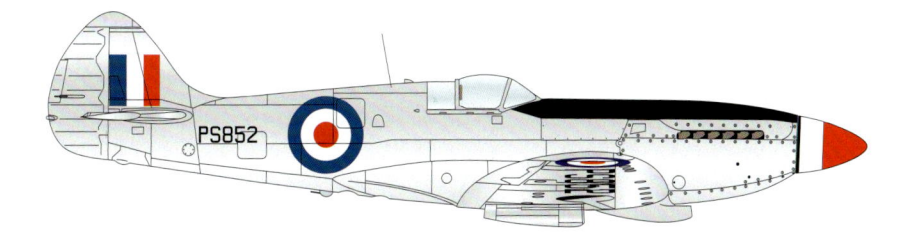

SPITFIRE EVOLUTION

FINALE

By 1944, it was clear that the days of the piston-engined day fighter were numbered. Five years earlier, the Air Ministry had started working in the highest secrecy on a jet-engined fighter programme which would lead to the Gloster Meteor becoming the only Allied jet aircraft in service during the Second World War.

At Supermarine, the parent company, Vickers, was keen to extract every last ounce of development from the Spitfire design. The last of the specialist photo-reconnaissance versions, the Mk XIX had entered service and was achieving excellent results over Germany.

This development was to take the Mk IV airframe, used to develop the Griffon engine in November 1941 and to examine upgrading the C Wing to take a mock-up of six Hispano cannon. The prototype was re-designated the Mk XX to avoid confusion with the re-designated PR Mk IV (which had been the PR Mk Id). It gets a little more convoluted when the Mk XX was re-designed again, this time to see through the Mk XII development.

The second Mk XX prototype flew in August 1942 with a Griffon II and then, in December 1942, it was re-engined with the Griffon 61. Nomenclature was never a strong point of Supermarine – remember the Spitfire going to be called the Shrew – so now, this Mk XX became the first Mk 21. By now, the Air Ministry had decided to drop Roman numerals for Arabic ones too.

The Spitfire F 21 prototype had been ordered by the Ministry of Aircraft Production in a contract worth £ 14,734 placed in 1944 in an effort to

---

Spitfire Mk 21
LA329, 'RAG.J' of No 600 (City of London) Squadron, RAuxAF, RAF Biggin Hill, 1945

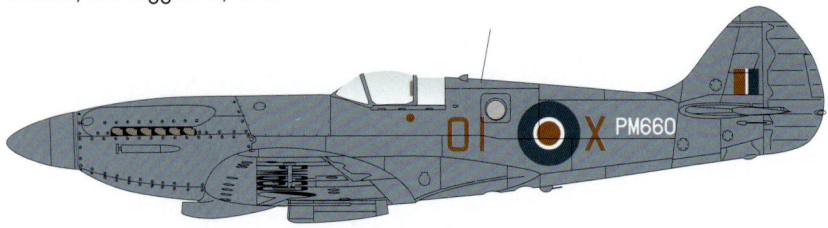

Spitfire Mk F 22
PK599, 'RAT.K' of No 613 (City of Manchester)
Squadron, RAuxAF, RAF Ringway, 1949

Spitfire Mk F 24
VN489, 'W2.A' of No 80 Squadron, RAF,
RAF Kai Tak, Hong Kong, 1950

revitalise the Spitfire, completely re-designed the wing to improve the flying characteristics which had been poor in initial flight trials. Aileron reversal at high speeds had been encountered and it was decided that the Shenstone elliptical wing had run its course.

Hursley Park pulled out the stops in this last evolutionary step by replacing the Faddy/Clifton wing structure, including upgraded skin (cladding), enlarging the ailerons and standardising the armament to two Hispano II 20 mm cannon in each wing; the day of the machine was over. The F 21 kept the high back of the Mk XII although it had many of the features of the Mk XIV in early examples at Castle Bromwich. Despite a very negative report on the F 21 from the Air Fighting Development Unit, which went as far as to recommend that development of the Spitfire should stop, there were two more day fighter marks to come after the 122 of this mark.

It is worth recording that the F 21 entered service in January 1945, by

South Marston operated as an out-station of Castle Bromwich for the fabrication of the Seafire Mk 22. It was also part of the Civilian Repair Organisation with outstanding engineering skills retained throughout the Second World War.

The Spiteful was the design which Supermarine hoped would replace the Spitfire. It had a number of features needed in the Spitfire, like a wide-track undercarriage. Even with a new laminar-flow wing, it was clear that Spitfire evolution had run its course.

which time the *Luftwaffe* had almost ceased to exist as an effective fighter force. The only known claim was Kriegsmarine midget submarine caught on the surface.

Basically identical to the F 21, the penultimate Spitfire was the F 22. The high back fuselage had been cutaway and a tear drop canopy applied to all the 260 produced at Castle Bromwich. Later aircraft, certainly the 27 completed at South Marston, were fitted with the tail fin and rudder which had been developed for the Spiteful, the planned Spitfire successor.

After the Second World War, the F 22 became the mainstay of the Royal Auxiliary Air Force with 12 squadrons, joining the single regular unit, it based in Malta. By 1955, all were retired, returned to Vickers at Chilbolton and sold on to Egypt, Southern Rhodesia and Syria.

The Mk 23 was a planned version, later called the Supermarine Valiant which was intended to have better performance in the dive and high speed flight. A Mk VIII was taken in hand but it seems never reached production.

The final Spitfire land-based day fighter was the F 24 under a Vickers Armstrong contract for 54 units at £ 7,100 each and to be delivered between February 1946 and March 1948 from the Castle Bromwich and South Marston factories. A further 27 airframes were converted from the F 22, mainly by improving the flying surfaces and trim arrangements. This Spitfire served from 1948 to 1952 with No 80 Squadron but continued in service in Hong Kong until 1955.

It is worth reflecting that the F 24 was twice as heavy, twice as powerful and climbed 80 % faster than the Mk I just a decade before, thanks to the Rolls-Royce Griffon.

Spiteful prototype, 1946
Test flown at High Post immediately after the Second World War, the Spiteful was considered such a departure for Spitfire evolution that the name Victor was allocated to it if it reached production.

EVOLVING WEBBED FEET

Even before the Spitfire had entered service with the Royal Air Force, the Fleet Air Arm of the Royal Navy was briefed by Fairey Aviation with a plan to build a naval version for carrier use. The Admiralty, never a great supporter of aviation even after winning back control of 'organic' aviation the year before, did not want to invest and the idea was dropped.

After the outbreak of the Second World War, the Admiralty, with Vice Admiral Sir Guy Royle, a former aircraft carrier captain, replacing Admiral The Hon Sir Alexander Ramsey as Fifth Sea Lord and responsible for aviation, took another look. The Air Ministry allowed a Spitfire Mk Ia to be flown by Lieutenant Commander A C G Ermen and after discussions with Supermarine's

Seafire Mk Ib
PA103, 'AC.B' of 736 NAS based at
RNAS St Merryn, September 1943

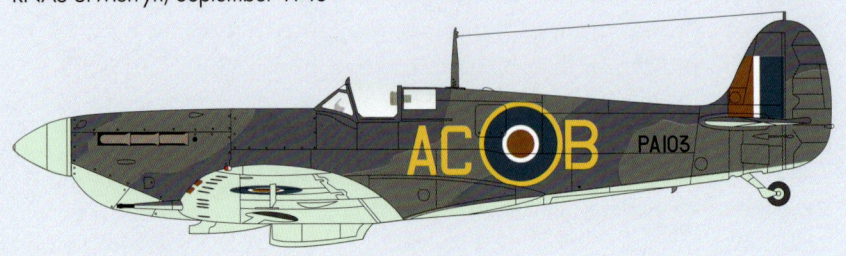

Seafire Mk Ib (Trop)
MB366, 'K' of 801 NAS aboard HMS *Furious*,
during Operation Torch, November 1942

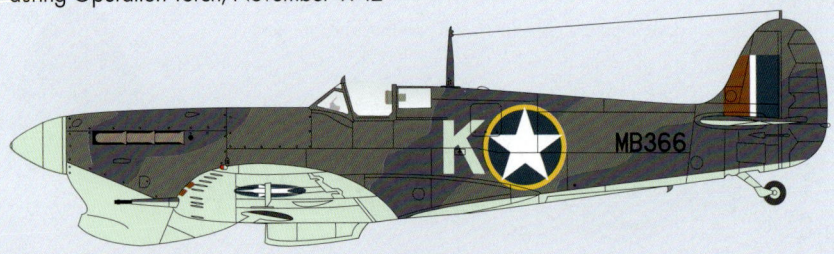

SPITFIRE EVOLUTION

This Castle Bromwich-built Spitfire Mk Vb was converted at Hamble to Seafire Mk Ib standard with an A-frame hook and tropic filter to help cope with salt-saturated air.

Seafire Mk IIc
MB183, '7.T' of 880 NAS aboard HMS *Argus*,
Home Fleet, October 1942

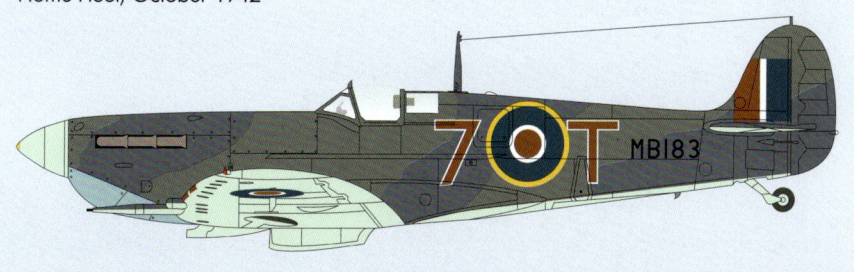

Seafire Mk L IIc
LR755 of The Fighter Flight, 843 NAS based at
Puttalam, Ceylon, March 1944

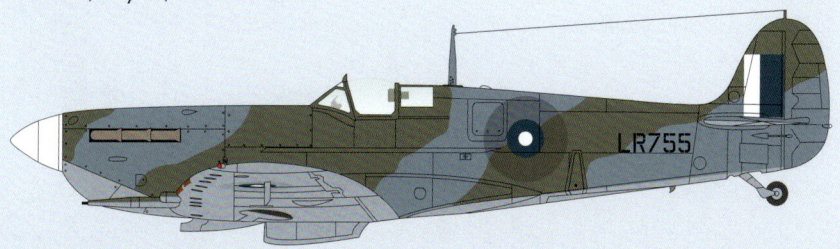

SPITFIRE EVOLUTION   61

acting chief designer, Joe Smith, discovered that plans were already underway for a 'hooker Spitfire'.

Winston Churchill, the First Lord of the Admiralty (a political appointment) was offered 50 navalised Spitfires with hooks and folding wings in February 1940 by Sir Kingsley Wood, the Secretary of State for Air, but rejected the offer.

It was not until late 1941 that the Ministry of Aircraft production allowed the Admiralty to assess the Spitfire and made 48 Spitfire Mk Vb airframes available for conversion by Air Training Services Ltd at Hamble, conveniently close to Supermarine and already a Spitfire sub-contractor.

Strengthening work was carried out on the rear fuselage including the longerons to carry the weight and stress of the A-frame hook for stopping the Seafire's landing run, by catching arrestor wires on a carrier's flight deck. Trials by Jeffrey Quill and Sub-Lieutenant Eric Brown had proved that more strengthening was needed. This did not stop 118 Seafire Mk Ibs being ordered from Cunliffe-Owen, across the airfield from Supermarine at Eastleigh. The first were delivered to the Fleet Air Arm in June 1942.

Refining the requirement and the design led to Supermarine and Westland Aircraft being given contracts for the Seafire Mk IIc. This was a Spitfire Mk Vc with catapult spools, a slinging lug or crane transfer, and the option to improve the power plant. Three versions were created: Seafire F Mk IIc and FR Mk IIc with the Marlin 46 engine and the L Mk IIc with a Merlin 32, which had been created for the Fleet Air Arm. All these variants had a four-bladed Rotol airscrew with improved deck clearance. In February 1943, Eric Brown also carried out trials with the Seafire Mk II small rocket motors attached either side to wing root to improve hot and heavy take-off performance from a short deck.

Seafire Mk IIc (Hybrid)
Seafire Mk IIc (Hybrid) LR792, 'K/Betty' flown by Lieutenant D.A.E. Holbrook of 834 NAS aboard HMS *Battler*, British East Indies Fleet, Indian Ocean, June 1944

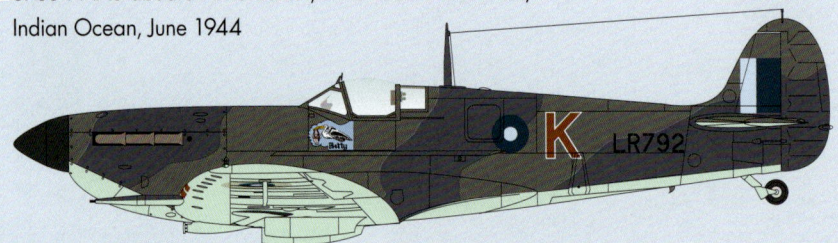

PHOTOGRAPHED ON LOCATION RIZONJET, BIGGIN HILL, KENT.

BLACK ★ STAR

SPITFIRE PR
SECRET

Date	Aircraft Type and No.	Crew	Duty	Details of Sortie and Flight	Reference
17.5.43	SPITFIRE EN 343.	F/O. FRAY. F.G.	PHOTO RECON.	OBJECTIVE - AREA, (MOHNE DAM - EDER DAM - SORPE DAM). RESULT - Photographs obtained of, MOHNE & SORPE DAMS.	D/578

OPERATIONS BOOK

BLACK STAR **SPITFIRE P.R. T-SHIRT**
£30/CAD$60

FIND OUT MORE **WWW.BLACKSTARBRANDS.COM**

ADAPTING THE SEAFIRE

Early marks of Seafire were adequate for interim use aboard an aircraft carrier, but the limited space and the need to strike down aircraft for maintenance and repair, required evolving the Seafire design to including folding wings. Joe Smith was firmly in the driving seat at Supermarine by the time the Seafire Mk III was on the drawing board; he worked with the Royal Aircraft Establishment at Farnborough to perfect the folding wings and the complex hinges.

Again three variants of the Mk III were created for three specific roles and used the Merlin 55 and its derivative, the Merlin 55M with the same Rotol airscrew as the Mk II. New exhausts and provision for external fuel were added; these modifications made to the Spitfire could be easily incorporated.

Westland and Cunliffe-Owen manufactured over a thousand Seafire Mk IIs, many with the new Hispano Mk V cannon which was lighter and shorter than the Mk II. It had been proved on the Spitfire and was easily incorporated in the Seafire.

Seafire Mk III
PP979, 'D.5X' of 807 NAS aboard HMS *Hunter*, British East Indies Fleet, Andaman Sea, May 1945

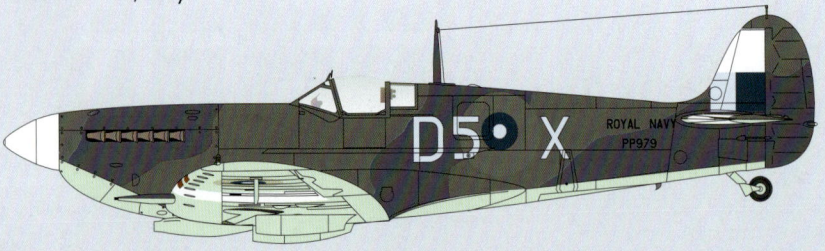

Most numerous of the Seafire variants, the Mk III had z-fold
wings and many were produced by Westland Aircraft.

Seafire Mk L III
PR189, 'P7.N' of 801 NAS aboard HMS *Implacable*, British Pacific Fleet,
8th Carrier Air Group, circa May 1945

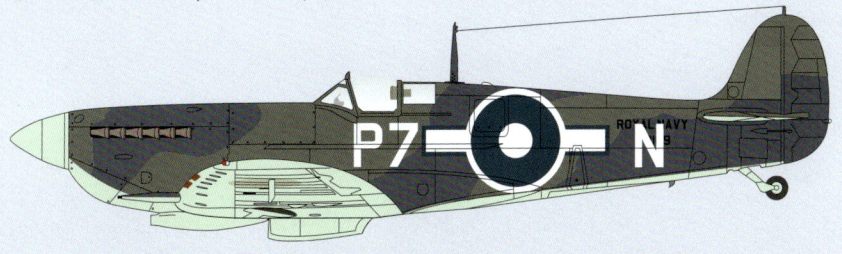

Seafire Mk FR III
NN621, '115/N' flown by Lieutenant Commander R. 'Mike' Crosley,
DSC of 880 NAS aboard HMS *Implacable*, British Pacific Fleet,
8th Carrier Air Group, May 1945

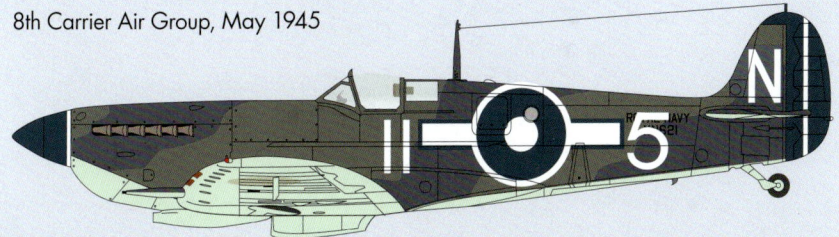

SPITFIRE EVOLUTION 65

ENTER THE GRIFFON II

Nomenclature was not, apparently, Supermarine's forte, nor that of the Ministry of Aircraft Production. Confusing the system with the out of sequence Seafires Mk I, Mk II and Mk III, the next variant was the Mk XV which took Spitfire Mk VII, Mk XII and Seafire Mk III attributes and combined them with the Griffon VI engine with its single-stage supercharger.

The first Griffon-powered Seafire, the Mk XV, was, however, back in sequence with the Spitfire. Built to specification N4/43, this model of the Seafire incorporated the traditional sting-type arrestor hook which again required structural work. It was rated a success yet only 390 were built by Cunliffe-Owen after six prototypes had been built by Supermarine.

On testing, Lieutenant Eric Brown commented on its unfortunate propensity

Seafire Mk XV
Serial unknown, '122' of 806 NAS aboard
HMS *Glory*, 16th Carrier Air Group, September 1946

Seafire Mk XV
SR530, 'AA.K' of 883 Squadron, RCN based
at RCNAS Dartmouth, June 1948

to 'hop across the deck' and tendency to drift towards the aircraft carrier's island superstructure when power was applied to the 1,850 hp Griffon. Again, a RATOG system was offered to negate the need for full power on take-off but most pilots preferred the risk of a torque swing to starboard to an asymmetric firing of the rockets.

On advice from the Royal Aircraft Establishment, Joe Smith proposed strengthening the Mk XV's undercarriage to alleviate the hopping motion and making more of the tear drop canopy and cut down rear fuselage. The Seafire was evolving just like the Spitfire had done, but about 12 months behind. Together with the increased fuel capacity (an extra 33 Imp gal), the Seafire Mk XVII (later designated Mk 17) was produced at Yeovil by Westland Aircraft and a small number at Eastleigh by Cunliffe-Owen, so that 232 eventually came off the two lines. It remained with the Royal Naval Volunteer Reserve's Air Wing until 1950 and was highly regarded by its pilots and engineers.

Seafire Mk XVII
SX273, 'S5.0' of 741 NAS, Operational Flying Training Unit, Air Warfare School based at RNAS St Merryn, early 1947

Seafire Mk XVII
SX336, built by Westland Aircraft in 1946 and re-built by Kennet Aviation at North Weald nearly 60 years later.

INTERIM GRIFFON SEAFIRE

With the availability of the Rolls-Royce Griffon 60 series, it was natural that the Fleet Air Arm should examine bringing it together into an evolved navalised Spitfire Mk 21, even at a cost of non-folding wings. The Mk 45 was a post-war development with improved fuel capacity and it went to the training unit, 778 Naval Air Squadron, in November 1946. It was clear that the piston-engined fighter's days were numbered when only 50 were built in the final days of the Castle Bromwich Aircraft Factory.

Fitting two F24 cameras in the rear fuselage in about a dozen of the Mk 45 airframes gave the Royal Navy the ability to undertake reconnaissance of foreign climes outside the range of land-based aircraft. These few were designated FR Mk 45.

Seafire Mk 45
LA486, '583/LP' of 771 NAS, 51st Miscellaneous Air Group,
RNAS Lee-on-Solent, summer 1950

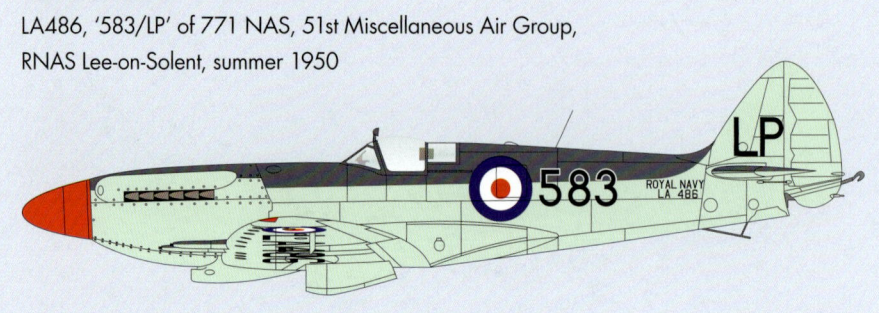

Seafire Mk 46
LA546, '900/LM' flown by Captain (Later Admiral) Caspar John
of the Station Flight, RNAS Lossiemouth, early 1948

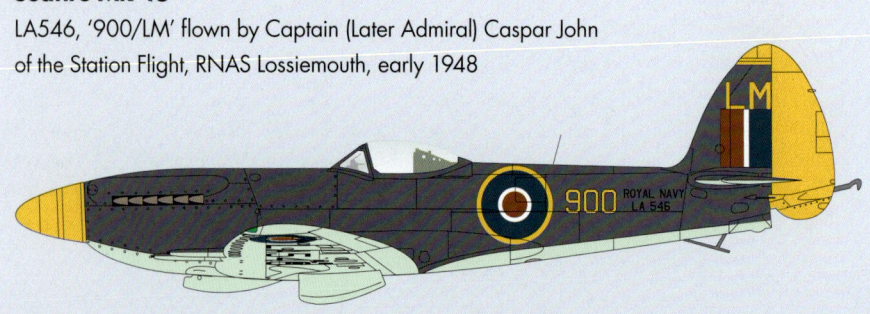

Demonstrating the contra-rotating propeller fitting, this South Marston-built Seafire F Mk 46 shows penultimate lines of the Spitfire/Seafire evolution.

It was also natural that the Spitfire F22 should also morph into a Seafire variant with tear drop canopy and cut down rear fuselage. An uprated Griffon 61/64 was fitted, driving a five-bladed Rotol airscrew and some were fitted with the Griffon 85/87 to power a Rotol contra-rotating design to eliminate torque issues on launch and recovery. The Spiteful/Seafang tail was incorporated after engineering work at High Post and Chattis Hill.

This all led to a competent naval aeroplane but one which has no longer relevant. Of the 240 ordered from Supermarine, only 24 were completed. The Mk 46 can also be seen as the prototype for the last of the evolutionary line, the Seafire Mk 47.

Seafang Mk 31, 1946

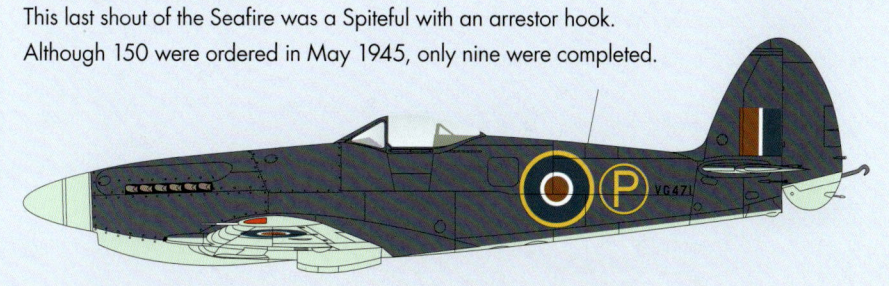

This last shout of the Seafire was a Spiteful with an arrestor hook. Although 150 were ordered in May 1945, only nine were completed.

SPITFIRE EVOLUTION

ULTIMATE & DEFINITIVE

Naval fighter pilots rejoice in the fact that the royal Navy deployed two fighter types to the Korean War and that the Royal Air Force had to make do with a few seconded pilots to the US and Royal Australian Air Forces.

First on the scene were the Seafire Mk 47 fighters of 800 Naval Air Squadron, which had been operated off Malaya during the Communist Emergency there in 1949. Due to sail home, the aircraft carrier HMS *Triumph*, with 800 embarked, turned left out of Singapore and headed to the Yellow Sea to join the United Nations attempting to stem the tide of Communist aggression against South Korea.

This was in so many ways the swansong of the Spitfire/Seafire evolution. The Mk 47 had no prototype but brought together lessons and ideas from Hursley Park into two trials aircraft. Very much a last throw of the dice, with all the refinements that RAE, the Royal Navy and Supermarine had ever wanted, the Seafire Mk 47 featured hydraulically-powered folding wings, a modified Seafire Mk XVII windscreen (which actually proved less than a success because it made life difficult for flight deck landings) and a huge contra-rotating airscrew. Another modification, the long supercharger air duct for the late model Griffon, improved engine performance but limited airspeed, especially in the climb.

Seafire Mk 47 fighters were withdrawn from Korea in 1951 after a friendly-fire incident with American bombers and when peacetime airworthiness rules were re-imposed. When HMS *Triumph* returned home, all of the type joined the Royal Naval Reserve, continuing to service until 1953.

Seafire Mk 47
VP461, '178/P' of 800 NAS, 13th Carrier Air Group aboard HMS *Triumph* off North Korea, August 1950

The last Mk 47 – and the last Spitfire or Seafire – left the Supermarine line on 28 January 1949, making the type the only Allied type in production throughout the 1939-45 Second World War. In all, 90 F Mk 47 and FR Mk 47 (again fitted with the F24 camera) were built.

The last words are with Eric Brown. "The Seafire 47 was simply thunderous."

Marked for the Korean War with high visibility stripes (which did not stop a USAF B-29 shooting one down), the Seafire Mk 47 was the last of the breed to engage in operations in contested airspace.

Philip Makanna's camera has caught the Seafire Mk 47 which has been restored to its 804 Naval Air Squadron markings which she wore in 1948. She was assembled at South Marston and restored at Booker airfield.

SPITFIRE EVOLUTION

ACKNOWLEDGEMENTS

This book has set out to identify the many variants and versions of the Spitfire and Seafire. To explain the numbering system, which is best described as byzantine in its complexity. It builds on *Spitfire People*, the examination of the unsung heroes of the Supermarine Type 300 development. That development went all the way to the Seafang, and, it could be argued, to the early naval jets.

To make this book appear at all has required a number of friends and supporters helping out during an incredibly short development and production period. The artist Jon Freeman has produced excellent drawings, some of which have already appeared on posters and some of my other publications, but the new ones maintain his high standard. Richard Parsons has used flair and genius to design the book to be accessible and coherent. Wing Commander John Davis, a legend himself in the delivery of air shows, has helped with the reading and syntax, as has my wife Cate. My son, Jack, the budding pilot, has been the resident 'spotter' on variant configuration control. There are only a few pictures but I would like to thank Philip Makanna at GHOSTS and John Goodman for their help and permissions.

Bulpitt Printing in Andover has produced the beautifully finished, perfect-bound product and my friends in the publishing world will help with distribution of what is the first book of Beaver Westminster Limited as a publisher.

I have been pointed in the right direction several times by Captain Eric Brown and David Faddy, the son of Alf Faddy, who has also kindly contributed the foreword. At the Kemble Roundel of the Spitfire Society, Joy Lofthouse and Judy Mansbridge Munger have offered the advice and criticism that every writer needs. Alfie Southwell has been cheering from the side-lines, as ever!

In the end, of course, the preceding 70 pages are my responsibility. If you see something in error, please contact me; until then, happy reading.

Paul Beaver
February 2016